THE OUTPOURING

VOLUME ONE

"To Experience The Holy Spirit As Sons And Daughters Of Our Heavenly Father."

RICHARD SCOTT BROWN

WOW Book Publishing™

Copyright © 2022 – Richard Scott Brown

WOW Book Publishing™

Unless otherwise indicated, all Scripture references are from the King James Version of the Holy Bible. All poems included in this book were written by the author. All rights reserved. This book is protected under copyright laws. This book may not be copied or reprinted for commercial gain or profit. The use of short quotations or occasional page copying for personal, or group study is permitted and encouraged.

Please note that this publishing style capitalises certain pronouns and words from the Holy Bible. Words such as Heavenly Father, Holy Spirit, Holy Ghost, Lord Jesus Christ, Son, Scripture, Name of Jesus etc.

Dedication

I was inspired to write this book to help others discover their identity in the Lord Jesus Christ as sons and daughters of our Heavenly Father. To challenge those who have not yet accepted Christ as their Lord and saviour to come into the fold before it's too late.

This book is especially dedicated to the people who I love and live with, my beautiful wife Anthonette and our three beautiful princesses, Richelle, Abigail and Esther-Rose.

This book is also dedicated to my parents (George Brown and Pauline Gray), my siblings, Christopher Brown, and Monique Brown. To my extended family (uncles, aunties and cousins) all over the globe, but special mention must go to the Marr family in London for the role you've played in my life since I've been living in the UK. Aunty Daphne, you've been another mother to me and Stuart Marr you've proven to be a friend and a brother from another mother since we attended Ewarton Primary School.

To all my in-laws (mother-in-law aka Mommy Betty, sister-in-law and brother-in-law), aunties, uncles, cousins, school, college, and University mates. God bless you all.

To the late Veronica-Francis Leigh (a friend and sister in Christ) and Dr Sonia King (a friend, work colleague and sister in Christ), I can't help but mention you both. As you rest in eternal peace, I'm confident you'd be very proud of my accomplishments. You both were always encouraging me and you were always intrigued to know when I'll be publishing my first book. Dr King your last words to me was "God is faithful and true, give Him honour at all times.

I also dedicate this book to all those who will not only find their identity in Christ as sons and daughters but will be able to access and walk in the authority and power that God has given to us. To all the prodigal sons and daughters who will find their way back home in the fold, to all those who are far off and as many as the Lord God shall call.

Love In Christ,
Richard Scott Brown

Table of Contents

Acknowledgement ix
What Others Are Saying xiii
Foreword xxi
Introduction 1

Chapter 1
Man Was Made In God's Image And Likeness 7
    Loving God and Loving Our neighbours 7
    What Is Man That Thou Art Mindful of Him? 13
    Trichotomy Man vs Dichotomy Man 19
    The Body 23
    The Soul 23
    The Spirit 24
    Understanding Who We Are 26
    Spiritual Authority Given to Adam At Creation 27

Chapter 2
The Fall Of Man 31
    Disobedience to God's Word 32
    We Are Tempted By Our Own Lusts 37

    Lust of The Flesh 44

    Lust of The Eyes 46

    The Pride of Life 47

    The Temptation of Jesus Christ 49

    Evicted from The Garden (God's Presence) 56

    The Canopy of Your Love 58

Chapter 3
The Need For A Spiritual Regeneration 61

    The Spirit of God Leaving King Saul 61

    Please Don't Take Your Spirit From Me 65

    You Must Be Born again 72

    Born of The Water 75

    Born of the Spirit 88

    The Untangling Of My Chains 92

Chapter 4
The Valley Of Dry Bones Experience 95

    Valley of Dry Bones (spiritual cemetery) 96

    Very Many In the Open Valley 98

    Can These Bones Live? 102

    Prophesy- Hear The Word of The Lord 104

    God Will Cause His Breath To Enter Into You
To Live Again 107

    I Will Open Your Graves 111

Chapter 5
Sons And Daughters Of Our Heavenly Father 115
   God Sons in Scripture 115
   Who Am I? (My Origin, Destiny and Purpose) 118
   Power to become the sons of God 120
   Without the Spirit of Christ, we are none of His 124
   The Sons of God are led by the Holy Spirit 126
   Creation is awaiting the manifestation of
   the sons of God 133
   Thou Mighty Man of Valour 138
   Come out from among them 140

Chapter 6
I Will Pour Out My Spirit Unto You 147
   The promise of the Holy Spirit in Joel 147
   The promise of the Holy Spirit in Proverbs 153
   Day of Pentecost 157
   The need for our understanding to be opened
   to the Scriptures 168
   Who do you say That I the Son of man am? 178

Conclusion 193
Bibliography 197
About The Author 201

Acknowledgement

Writing this book, The Outpouring- To Experiencing The Holy Spirit as Sons and Daughters of Our Heavenly Father, has been a very significant journey for me and so has been my life. I could not have attained to any level of success without the contribution of key people at different stages of my journey both in a secular educational setting and my Christian community. Most Importantly, the guiding and comforting presence of the Holy Spirit. Who is the Head of my life, throughout my Christian walk for over thirty years, as a son of the Most High God.

It is for this reason I want to show gratitude to the men and women who have had a positive impact on my life. I will not be able to mention everyone, (you know yourselves and how much you've impacted my life) because that will become an additional chapter. Some of them are still alive, while others are no longer with us.

To the late Mrs Vera Williams (Miss V). My brother and I were left in your care for over three years when our mother was out working. You took very good care of us and taught us Godly principles. The late Bishop Neville Hamilton. You were a very good example of what a Pastor should be. It was under your leadership I became a born-again Christian at the age of 15. You poured into me when I needed it most. As you rest in eternal peace, let it be known that apart of your legacy lives on in me. Also, to your family and members of the Ewarton Gospel Lighthouse Church past and present, wherever I go you have a special place in my heart.

My former Sunday School teacher at the Ewarton Gospel Lighthouse, the late Dorothy Labeach, and your family. Thank you for the deeds of kindness and words of encouragement you've shown towards me over the years. To My aunty Vicky (Miss Nellie Brown), you've been like a second mother to me over the years. People see me and don't know the significant role you've played in my brother and I upbringing. God bless you richly.

To Bishop Joslyn Williams, family and brethren of Emmanuel Apostolic Church, Snow Hill, Portland, Jamaica. May God continue to bless and keep you and your family Bishop Williams. God used you as a vessel of honour and an intercessor as you came to my rescue, in the pouring rain, at one of the lowest points in my life. Many people don't even know this.

To Bishop John Francis, your wife, and the entire Leadership, and friends at Ruach City Church. My life was greatly impacted being a member of this Ministry for over 12 years. Bishop Omroy Miller and brethren of Sozo Ministry International. God used you to help me along my journey. For this I'm grateful. Pastor Blackman and the entire family of Shekinah House of Praise, your prophetic

Acknowledgement

words of encouragement and effective fervent prayers for my family and I have been acknowledged. To Apostle Winston Baker, the leadership and brethren of King Jesus Pentecostal Fellowship in Jamaica, and the rest of the world. Your Ministry has impacted me at a time when I most needed it. It wasn't a coincidence but a God-incident when I stumbled across it on Facebook in 2019. To Bishop James Herbert, the leadership, mothers in Zion and brethren of Life and Light Fellowship Church. Thanks for your prayers and encouragement for my family and me. It is much appreciated. To all my friends at New Testament Church of God (George Street Birmingham), memories of our beautiful wedding still live on.

Finally, to all my teachers and lecturers who have taught and impacted my life tremendously across different institutions since the age of three. These institutions include Ewarton Gospel Lighthouse Basic School, Ewarton Primary School, Charlemont High School, Sydney Pagon STEM Academy (formerly Elim Agricultural School), College of Agriculture, Science and Education (CASE) and The UCL Institute of Education.

There are two very important people who have been of tremendous support to me since I migrated to the United Kingdom. Firstly, Miss Vervaline Williams (Aunt Lyn), from the very first day you have only shown me kindness. You are like a grandmother to me. Secondly, Mrs Mavis Findley. You have always said I'm like a son you didn't have. You have always encouraged me in my Christian walk. You came to my rescue at a very low point in my life (I was evicted and would have had nowhere to live). May God continually bless and keep you both.

Last but not least, I want to acknowledge Keisha Cummings of Koffee Radio in Atlanta USA. By God, you gave me an avenue to share the Gospel of Jesus Christ in Radio Land every Sunday morning. My beloved sister in Christ, Mary Atere, God has used you many times to encourage me on this journey. Sister Deion Grant-Ferguson of the Prayer Clinic, thank you for being led by the Holy Spirit to ask me to Minister during Pentecost, that's how this book was born. To the founder of Wow Book Camp Mr Vishal Morjaria you have taught me well and the supporting cast of Book Angels in particular Mr Samuel Kitenge.

What Others Are Saying

In **Psalms 107:1** David said, *"Oh, give thanks to the LORD, for He is good! For His mercy endures forever."* After reviewing a portion of this book, I felt inspired to use the verse mentioned above to express my appreciation to the author for the authenticity of content. This book magnifies the purpose for which Jesus Christ came into the world… "To save us from our sins".

Aspects of the content points us to the Sovereignty of God, the importance of obeying God and the consequences of disobedience. It also beautifully expands and expounds on Jesus's declaration to Nicodemus in St. John 3:5 "Most assuredly, I say to you, unless one is born of water and the Spirit, he cannot enter the kingdom of God". I therefore find the information outlined in this chapter very relevant to those who are seeking the Salvation offered to sinners by Jesus Christ, need to know about **Spiritual Regeneration** and for those seeking to access resource information on the topic for sermons purposes or for teaching.

I pray that the Holy Spirit will continue to inspire and guide the Author as he avails himself to be an instrument in God's hand in achieving the divine objective of God's Amazing Grace.

—**Bishop Joslyn Williams (JP).**
General Secretary, Emmanuel Apostolic United Church of Christ Int.
Pastor, Emmanuel Apostolic Church.
Snow Hill Portland, Jamaica

This book is very good and informative. The readers will definitely be blessed.

Joel chapter two is one of my favourite Scriptures in the Old Testament that really show how the Holy Spirit was very active. We see how the Holy Spirit was very much involved in creation as He moved across the face of the waters (**Gen 1:2**). The Holy Spirit communicated the Father's message to His children to put us in alignment so that we can receive the Father's blessing.

As you read this book, you are going to get a good understanding of what true repentance is and what it will produce in your life. The outpouring of the Holy Spirit as explained in this book, will cause a stirring in your spirit to seek the face of God which will result in an outpouring of the Holy Spirit and activation of the gifts that have been dormant in your life.

—**Bishop Karel Gray.**
Senior Pastor, New Life Pentecostal Ministries, Inc
New Jersey, USA

What Others Are Saying

We were very much privileged and honoured to have had the opportunity at Agape Church, to pre-launch this book "The Outpouring- To Experience The Holy Spirit As Sons and Daughters of Our Heavenly Father," authored by Richard Scott Brown. This we did as we were led by the Holy Spirit. Our Church was blessed by the excellent presentation and teaching by Richard Scott Brown. To the extent we are planning to translate this book in our language for us to use as a teaching resource for the local churches.

We've also requested and have arranged for Richard Scott Brown to do a six-month series of teaching under the heading End Times because we see this book containing great End Time Information for the Church. He will teach once per month to our church in Rawalpindi from one Chapter per month from February to July 2022. We believe this wonderful book will benefit the growth of believers and non-believers. This book will teach us how we can get ready for the second coming of Christ. There are six Chapters in this book and every Chapter is key to bringing about change and success in our lives. We can learn who we are, where we came from and where we are going. As you read this book your faith will grow to a new level in Jesus Christ.

—**Pastor Anil Yousuf**
Agape Church, Rawalpindi Pakistan

I was honoured to have had the opportunity to review a portion of this book in its pre-publishing state. I have found it to be very inspiring, convicting and soul searching at the same time. I love it and I pray all who read this book will have the same and even a greater experience.

It has been a wonderful privilege as the leader and founder of Shekinah House of Praise Ministry to be affiliated with this humble young man of God, Richard Scott Brown. I've known him to be a prolific writer and preacher of the Gospel of Jesus Christ, which has been a blessing to many.

A known carrier of the power of the Word of God under the direction of the Holy Spirit. A devoted prophet of God, husband, and father of three to whom God has invested His word, wisdom, and delight. Richard Scott Brown's passion and mission goal is to spread the Gospel of Jesus Christ to the end of the earth by proclaiming the power of God according to **Acts 6:8**. In addition, this man of God is well loved by many ministerial persons both young and senior who have heard him preaching from all over the world.

On behalf of Shekinah House of Praise, we decree over your life according to **Jeremiah 29:11** "Though thy beginning was small, yet thy latter end shall greatly increase," In the Name of the Lord Jesus Christ.

—Maxeen Blackman
Senior Pastor, Shekinah House of Praise Ministry
London, UK

I was one of the honoured and privileged few who had the opportunity to review a portion of this book before it was published. The chapter I read was a very powerful, deep, and a profound exposition of the overwhelming love of God towards his people. During a time when the whole house of Israel turned away from God, they became dry and hopeless. However, God continues to show love, compassion, and mercy to his people. God spoke through Ezekiel to prophesy over his people to bring their dead state to life.

God can restore, renew, and revitalise anything that is dead. Wherever our heart is, that's where our desire will be and the more we feed it the stronger it grows. If we feed the flesh we will reap corruption, if we feed the spirit, we will receive eternal life. This will help individuals to be more rooted and grounded in God. For us to receive the outpouring, our vessels must be clean and live a life pleasing to God.

I love how you used the scriptures to bring across the message and how well it is put together and explained with clarity. I know the good news will spread and many will get a deeper understanding of what God is saying in this book. Bless you man of God, may this book spread all over the world and your heart receive the words.

During the time of Covid and Lockdown you came, and you ministered to us the Pentecost (Upper Room) Prayer Ministry under the anointing of God and many hearts were touched by the powerful words of God. You prophesied to the group that God is going to work mightily among us and that some will receive the baptism of the Holy Spirit. Within a week after you spoke, two individuals got filled with the Holy Spirit at the same time.

The presence of God moved on Pentecost like never before. For a few weeks the anointing sat upon us. I'm a living testimony, I felt the fire of God over my body until this day I still do. This reminds me of Acts 2 when the disciples were in the Upper Room and the Holy Spirit came upon them like fire. Since you've ministered God's word, many people have heard about the mighty work of God amongst us and are now a part of Pentecost (Upper Room) Prayer Ministry.

You have sacrificed your time and put forth the word of God on different media such as Facebook, YouTube and now your books and other platforms to reach the lost. This is to help others to understand the Word of God. May God in return continue to pour into you words of wisdom, knowledge and understanding.

—**Allicestair McKenzie**
Leader of Pentecost-The Upper Room (An Online Prayer Ministry)
Clarendon, Jamaica

God bless you My brother Richard,

Man, you can write!

The "Fall of Man", what a chapter that fully details the scriptural chronology of the fall of man. The Scriptural evidence presented and expounded on is compelling and really does open one's eyes. Topics such as 'Lust of the Flesh, Lust of the Eyes & The Pride of Life' really trigger reflective prayer of protection so that we do not fall victim.

The Temptation of Jesus Christ is an awesome in-depth narrative of what Jesus faced and clearly brings insight to how the devil brings the fight of temptation to us. Our victory is explicit, even more so due to how God has used you, Brother Richard to bring a revelation of how Jesus overcame and therefore we can overcome too. How encouraging and hope building.

What Others Are Saying

Brother Richard, you are a great teacher of the Word. Gifted to expound on God's word where the reader can easily capture the essence and purpose of God's word. We were evicted from the Garden (God's Presence), but God so loved the World.

It is clear that you have a gift, there have been regular enquiries as to when you are coming back. I have now had the opportunity to read three of your chapters that are so deep and rich in the Word and revelation. The sheer fact that you are being requested back on the Prayer Clinic is evidence that you have been granted the anointing to bring God's word with an impact to the hearer. It is written that Faith comes by hearing and hearing the Word of God, so to me it is evident that you ministering on the Prayer Clinic has ignited and stirred up the faith of those who have listened to the message God has given through you. I also want you to recite "The Canopy of Your Love" (one of the powerful yet beautiful poems you wrote and inserted in your books) the next time you come on. Simply beautiful.

We are in very sorrowful times, where the Word of God is being watered down and often presenting as powerless. Men's hearts are not always seekers of the truth of the Word or preach it for the conversion of the souls. God has gifted you with this ability to not only preach but to write that brings the focus to Him and His truth. He said my people perish through a lack of knowledge. I would say to people come, buy this book and be edified and equipped up in the knowledge of God. Hallelujah.

Thank you again for the privilege to have read through this Chapter.

—Deion Grant-Ferguson
Leader of The Prayer Clinic (An Online Ministry)
London UK

Minister Richard Scott Brown is a Teacher of the Word from his humble beginnings as one of our Team of Discipleship/New Believer's Teachers back in the early days of Ruach City Church. He has shown himself to be someone who has truly invested in what the Spirit of the Lord has gifted him with, and we are seeing the Fruits of his labour that you are now holding in your hands.

It is my Prayer that the Spirit of the Lord will breathe upon the Message within to bring the Life of Jesus Christ to those in the Highways and the Byways. At such a time as this we need more than ever before the Spirit of the Living God to hover over the darkness and the chaos that our world is experiencing to birth the supernatural Light and Life of Almighty God on the earth. We say Father God use this work from your Servant, for your Glory we pray.

Minister Richard we congratulate and celebrate your endeavours and trust the Holy Spirit to use it for the Advancing of the Kingdom to the Glory of God.

—**Enid Stewart (Resident Elder)** -
Brixton Location
Ruach City Church
London, UK

Foreword

In writing what is the first part of a two Volume series of an insightful and power packed books, The Outpouring-To Experience The Holy Spirit as Sons and Daughters of Our Heavenly Father. Richard has done a tremendous job in stimulating our faith to believe God for an End Time Revival and an Outpouring of His Spirit.

The Outpouring is a prophetic title and a well-named book about man who once operated in Spiritual authority and dominion that God gave them. Yet through disobedience they fell from grace and forfeited this Spiritual authority and dominion to Satan. For mankind to be restored to their first estate, they must realise the need for Spiritual Regeneration. This can only happen through water baptism and the baptism of the Holy Spirit. When these happen, mankind will once again operate not as subordinates, but as heirs & joint-heirs and as sons and daughters of our Heavenly Father.

It is very important for individuals to realise and understand who they are, and the purpose why they were created. If we fail to do so, we will underachieve and live a life that God did not intend for us to live. A life that is full of regrets and sorry. God loves the entire world and its His desire for all of us to recognise we can only achieve our ultimate goals in this life, only when we function as sons and daughters of our Heavenly. When we do this, we would have lived a life that brings Him glory and honour.

—**Vishal Morjaria**
Award winning Author & International Speaker
Wow Book Publishing

Introduction

When you look in the mirror what do you see? When you have a panoramic self-examination, do you see or feel God within yourself? Do you know who you are as an individual? Do you know how you came into existence? It is said if you don't know where you are coming from you won't know where you are going.

The Scriptures tell us that man was made in God's image and likeness. When people look at you, what or whose image are they seeing? We live in a world where image means a lot and most people are "image" conscious. Are you displaying God's image and likeness or are you portraying the image of a so-called superstar or some famous apparel brand? Is the image you are projecting one of success or failure, victory or defeat, boldness or timidity, power & authority, or fear?

There are many voices nowadays and many "thus says the Lord." Not every "thus says the Lord," is God speaking and not every voice we should heed to. The guide to be sure God is speaking is His word and the guidance of His Holy Spirit. The word of God and the Holy Spirit synchronise. It's full time we get back to having our steps completely ordered in God's word and to be led by the Holy Spirit as the sons and daughters of our Heavenly Father.

It was disobedience to God's word that led to the fall of man in the Garden of Eden. Who are we allowing to counsel us? Blessed is the man that walks not in the counsel of the ungodly or sits in the seat of the scornful, but his delight is in the law (word) of the Lord. Eve was deceived when she allowed Satan to twist God's word, to appease her fleshly desires. There is nothing wrong with God's word. It is still a lamp unto our feet and a light unto our path in the dark world we are living in. The Psalmist declares forever oh Lord thy word is settled (established) in Heaven. The Lord Jesus taught His disciples to pray "thy will be done in earth as it is done in Heaven." Just as how God's word is established in Heaven that's how His word should be established in our lives.

However, Satan wants us to think something is wrong with the Scriptures (Bible) and God's command. The moment we give him power to sow seeds of doubt in our mind concerning God's word we become vulnerable, and we become susceptible for a big fall. This is a dangerous place to be at. Like the Psalmist we must stand our ground and say thy word have I hid in my heart that I might not sin against thee.

The fall of man in the Garden of Eden resulted in both spiritual death and a natural death. Mankind became separated from their Creator. Sin resulted in Adam handing over the Spiritual authority God gave Him to Satan. To access this Spiritual authority and power which the Second Adam who was Jesus Christ won back, when He went into Hell and took the keys of death and Hell. We must experience a Spiritual Regeneration by becoming "born again," into God's Kingdom through water baptism in the Name of the Lord Jesus and being filled with the Holy Spirit. The Lord Jesus Christ said to Nicodemus marvel not that I say to you "you must be born again."

Like the Valley of Dry Bones in Ezekiel 37, God is looking to revive our spiritual man from a state of "spiritual death" to one where we become lively stones in His Church. As He had promised through the prophet Joel that in the Last Days He will pour out of His Spirit on all flesh. This promise was fulfilled on the Day of Pentecost but that was not the end of the promise. God declared that the glory of the latter house shall be greater than the glory of the former house. In this ending of the Last Days, God is looking to pour out even more that His sons and daughters can be effective witnesses as the Apostles did in Jerusalem and beyond, turning the known world upside down for the glory of God as they demonstrated the resurrection power of the Lord Jesus Christ. As they experienced that great "Outpouring," many souls were added to the Church of the Lord Jesus Christ daily.

This "Outpouring" is not for any and anyone but those who are obedient, willing to die to self, separate themselves from everything that isn't God, walk in God's commands, obedience to God's word fully (without adding or taking away from it), be subjected to the leading of the Holy Spirit, fast, pray and hunger and thirst after righteousness that they may be filled. God will only pour out of His Spirit on His sons and daughters who will in turn be led by the Holy Spirit to do God's perfect will.

I can't stress this enough, this outpouring doesn't necessarily depend on us "singing our favourite songs, or listening to our favourite worship leaders or preachers," but instead when we are walking in obedience to God's word. Since it was disobedience to God's word that led to the fall of man and eventually spiritual death, it's going to take obedience to God's word to bring this Outpouring and a great End Time Spiritual Revival.

A prerequisite to the day of Pentecost was the Apostles obeying the word of the Lord Jesus Christ to "tarry in Jerusalem until he be endowed with power from a high." God will never be desperate for us where He is going to twist or change His words to please us. His commands are eternal. Instead, He wants us to desire Him so much where we become desperate for Him and at whatever cost obey His commands.

If we are going to experience God's extraordinary Outpouring in these End Times, we must be willing to do something extraordinary. We cannot continue the same way, do the same things for doing sake and everything become ritualistic and become a religion and expect change. In this Outpouring God is looking for relationships and not the rituals of men and religion.

Revelation is key to having a relationship with the Lord Jesus Christ. God often reveals Himself through His word like He did to Samuel. Until God Himself opens our Understanding to understand His word, we will forever be in the dark as it relates to Scripture and walk in spiritual ignorance. We will read but not understand because the natural man doesn't understand the things of God because they are spiritually discerned. We will end up wrongly dividing the word of truth.

God is calling the End time Church to go back to go forward. Yes, God wants us to go back to the inception of the Church of the Lord Jesus Christ in the Book of the Acts of the Apostles and mirror how they operated. Until we get to a place where we will continue daily in the Apostles Doctrine, fellowship, breaking of bread, prayer, fasting, Holy communion, united (we can only be united when we are all doing the same things, singing from the same script as it is written in the Holy Scriptures, practice what the Apostles practice and teach, and are of the same Spirit), have all things in common, love each other especially those who are of the household of faith we will not experience the "Outpouring," that God so desires for us to experience in these the last days of the Last Day.

CHAPTER 1

Man Was Made In God's Image And Likeness

Man is a unique being. The last work in the creation of the world, man was formed in God's own image and likeness. Adam the first man (human being), was made from the dust (dirt, earth, soil) and was brought to life by God's breathing into his nostrils the breath of life. The Apostle Paul mentions Adam as the first man, a living soul in whom all die, and calls Christ the last Adam, a life-giving spirit in whom all is made alive.

Loving God and Loving Our neighbours

We are living in a time like never before, when people are so conscious of their image and identity. While some have understood and accepted who they are, there are those who appear to be confused or unacceptable about who they are, and are still searching for their "true" identity. Others have gone to the extent of changing their physical appearance in order that they may accept themselves in some form of physical capacity.

The two greatest commandments in scripture is for us to love the Lord God and love our neighbours. *Mark 12:29-33* *²⁹ And Jesus answered him, the first of all the commandments is, hear, O Israel; The Lord our God is one Lord: ³⁰ And thou shalt love the Lord thy God with all thy heart, and with all thy soul, and with all thy mind, and with all thy strength: this is the first commandment. ³¹ And the second is like, namely this, thou shalt love thy neighbour as thyself. There is none other commandment greater than these . . .*

Analysing the passage above, we will realise that in order for us to fulfil both commandments we are required to meet similar requirements. In the first commandment we are to love the Lord God with all ourselves (heart, soul, mind and strength). On the other hand, we are to love our neighbour as ourselves (body, soul and spirit).

Therefore, one can conclude that in order for us to love God and our neighbour, we must firstly understand who we are as individuals. That is knowing we have been made in the image and likeness of God, our bodies are the temple of the living God, with the purpose of bringing glory and honour to our Heavenly Father.

Secondly, we must love ourselves by seeing and valuing ourselves as God would see us. Not above or below how God sees us, if not, we will become lovers of self or operate below the standards God expects us to. There is a danger with becoming lovers of ourselves. When a person becomes a lover of themselves, they will also be; lovers of money, boastful, proud, abusive, disobedient to their parents, ungrateful, unholy, without love, unforgiving, slanderous, without self-control, brutal, not lovers of the good, treacherous, rash, conceited, lovers of pleasure rather than lovers of God. If we fail to understand ourselves and to love ourselves the way God intended to, we will fall short of meeting the requirements in order for the two greatest commandments to be fulfilled.

Just as in the natural world, if we want to have a very good look at ourselves we go and look in the mirror. Likewise, it's the same when it comes to spiritual matters. God's Word is that mirror that we should go to in order for us to understand who we truly are. **James 1:21-25** *[21] Therefore lay aside all filthiness and overflow of wickedness, and receive with meekness the implanted word, which is able to save your souls. [22] But be doers of the word, and not hearers only, deceiving yourselves. [23] For if anyone is a hearer of the word and not a doer, he is like a man observing his natural face in a mirror; [24] for he observes himself, goes away, and immediately forgets what kind of man he was. [25] But he who looks into the perfect law of liberty (God's Word) and continues in it, and is not a forgetful hearer but a doer of the work, this one will be blessed in what he does.*

God's Word has a mirror that enables us to see our true self, see our true condition, at the same time not leading us to a state of condemnation but if we practice what we read it will bring us to a place of salvation. Verse 21 states that the implanted word is able to save our souls.

Psalm 119:18,130 [18] *Open my eyes, that I may see wondrous things from Your law.* [130] *The entrance of Your words gives light; It gives understanding to the simple.*

The two verses above in **Psalm 119** highlights the revealing power of God's Word. Verse 18 states there are wondrous things in God's Law (His Word) for us to see. While verse 130 states that when we allow God's Word to enter the dark situations of our lives it will bring clarity and where wisdom and understanding were lacking God's Word will impart these, even in the simplest of individual's lives.

Going back to the point about meeting the requirements of fulfilling the two greatest commandments. That is, understanding ourselves and loving ourselves. To better understand ourselves as human beings let us have a deeper look into these verses. We are to love the Lord God with all our heart, soul, mind, and strength. That is, loving God with our entire being or self. Therefore, our heart, soul, mind, and strength constitute our being as humans.

If we want to love God, we will have to do so as He desires. We can't just naïvely design our own system of worship. The point Jesus was making about loving God with all our soul is that our lives need to be guided by God and intertwined with His way of life. Loving God with all our heart, soul, mind and strength requires us to die to our way of thinking, our will, desires and totally deny ourselves. Jesus taught in **Luke 9:23-25** [23] *And he said to them all, if any man will come after me, let him deny himself, and take up his cross daily, and follow me.* [24] *For whosoever will save his life shall lose it: but whosoever will lose his life for my sake, the same shall save it.*

²⁵ For what is a man advantaged, if he gains the whole world, and lose himself, or be cast away?

Our true love for God will be proven when we daily die to ourselves and devote all that we are and have to Him. All to the glory and honour of His Name. Until we die to ourselves, we won't form a genuine relationship with God. God is a Spirit, and it is only when our flesh is crucified, we can truly worship and connect to God in Spirit and in truth.

The writer of **Romans** states **12:1-2** *I beseech you therefore, brethren, by the mercies of God, that ye present your bodies a living sacrifice, holy, acceptable unto God, which is your reasonable service. ² And be not conformed to this world: but be ye transformed by the renewing of your mind, that ye may prove what is that good, and acceptable, and perfect, will of God.*

In proving our love for God, we present ourselves to Him daily as a living sacrifice, holy and acceptable. The word present reminds me of another word 'gift' that we used when we gave somebody something special on special occasions, for example a birthday. God wants us to offer ourselves as a gift or a present each day but on life's altar, we die daily to ourselves. Not only do we present our bodies, but we become transformed by having our minds renewed. Our mind is a powerful part of our being and in loving and living for God it must be renewed. It is by studying and meditating on God's words that our minds are going to be renewed. **Joshua 1:8** *⁸ This book of the law shall not depart out of thy mouth; but thou shalt meditate therein day and night, that thou mayest observe to do according to all that is written therein: for then* *thou shalt make thy way prosperous, and then thou shalt have good success.*

When we die to ourselves and have our minds renewed by God's word. We will begin to do things God's way, the end result is that God will make our way prosperous, and then we shall have good success.

Mankind has the capacity for life-function at three levels: body and soul and spirit. The apostle Paul prayed for the Thessalonian Christians that "the God of peace Himself might sanctify them entirely; and their spirit (pneuma) and soul (psuche)and body (soma) might be preserved completely, without blame at the coming of the Lord Jesus Christ" **(I Thess. 5:23)**. His desire was that Christians might be sanctified, might "be set apart to function as intended," at every level of their life-function, physical, psychological, and spiritual. This is what God intends for mankind.

Psalm 18:1-6 *I will love thee, O Lord, my strength.* [2] *The Lord is my rock, and my fortress, and my deliverer; my God, my strength, in whom I will trust; my buckler, and the horn of my salvation, and my high tower.* [3] *I will call upon the Lord, who is worthy to be praised: so shall I be saved from mine enemies . . .*

David declared his love for the Lord. Because of his love for the Lord, God was obligated to act on his behalf. In times of trouble God proved to be David's strength, rock, fortress, deliverer, buckler, horn of his salvation and his high tower. When we live a life that shows our love for God, there is so much that God will be to us, like He has been for David.

This goes to show that, when we are living for God, and loving Him it's not in vain. Loving the Lord is not lip service, but a life dedicated to Him through thick and thin, on the mountain top or down in the valley.

God is a God of covenant even to a thousand generations. In keeping our covenant with God, we will prove our love for Him. He will in turn fulfil His covenant to us. Like David when we call upon the Lord, who is worthy to be praised, we will be saved from our enemies. No matter what traps the enemy sets for us God will deliver us because we love Him. Even when we are compassed by the sorrows of death, when fear comes upon us God is there to deliver us. When we love God and trouble is steering us in our eyes, when we are distressed with different issues of life, God will always give an attentive ear to our cry. He will hear us from His temple, our tears won't be in vain. Because we love God our voice is distinct to Him and like the children of Israel, when we cry unto, He will send His word to heal us and deliver us from our destruction.

What Is Man That Thou Art Mindful of Him?

Psalm 8:3-6 *³ When I consider thy heavens, the work of thy fingers, the moon, and the stars, which thou hast ordained; ⁴ What is man, that thou art mindful of him? and the son of man, that thou visit him? ⁵ For thou hast made him a little lower than the angels, and hast crowned him with glory and honour. ⁶ Thou made him to have dominion over the works of thy hands; thou hast put all things under his feet:*

As we analyse the above passage, we realise that God has a deep interest in man. As the psalmist stated that you are mindful (watchful, attentive, aware), of him. God's eyes are forever on the lookout for mankind. Like the Prodigal son's father was daily being mindful, being on the lookout for his son to return home. **1 Peter 3:12** *[12] For the eyes of the Lord are over the righteous, and his ears are open unto their prayers: but the face of the Lord is against them that do evil.* **Psalm 32:8** *[8] I will instruct thee and teach thee in the way which thou shalt go: I will guide thee with my eye.* We mean so much to God, who is also our Heavenly Father, that each day His eyes are constantly watching us, His mind is full of us, and His ears are open to our prayers.

I want to encourage someone who doesn't feel worthy to be alive that those are not God's thoughts towards you. God is saying you are so special to the extent He is looking out for you, amidst there are over seven billion other people. God wants you to know that there is a purpose for your life, and He wants to have a relationship with you that is only possible through the Lord Jesus Christ. You are crying but it seems your tears are in vain. God wants you to cry out to Him instead. **Isaiah 65:24** *[24] And it shall come to pass, that before they call, I will answer; and while they are yet speaking, I will hear.* **Joel 2:32** *And it shall come to pass, that whosoever shall call on the name of the LORD shall be delivered: for in mount Zion and in Jerusalem shall be deliverance, as the LORD hath said, and in the remnant whom the LORD shall call.* God wants you to know that even before you call, He will answer and while you are still speaking He will hear you. That means He sees your heart. Pour out your heart to the Lord Jesus Christ. A broken and a contrite heart he will not despise. There is deliverance for you if you call upon the Name of the Lord Jesus Christ.

Not only are God's ears open to your cry, but He wants you to know He has lovely thoughts towards you to lead you to an expected end. **Jeremiah 29:11-13** [11] *For I know the thoughts that I think toward you, saith the Lord, thoughts of peace, and not of evil, to give you an expected end.* [12] *Then shall ye call upon me, and ye shall go and pray unto me, and I will hearken unto you.* [13] *And ye shall seek me, and find me, when ye shall search for me with all your heart.*

Compared to all of God's other creations, man has a special place in God's thoughts. Therefore, I believe the question that is being asked is this: "What is so special or unique about man that you can't help but to think of him." Man is so special to God that he was made a little lower than the angels. The reason for this special bond that God has for man is found in **Genesis 1:26-27** [26] *And God said, let us make man in our image, after our likeness: and let them have dominion over the fish of the sea, and over the fowl of the air, and over the cattle, and over all the earth, and over every creeping thing that creeps upon the earth.* [27] *So God created man in his own image, in the image of God created he him; male and female created he them.*

An image is as an exact likeness or a person strikingly like another person. Likeness is defined as the quality or state of being alike or similar, especially in appearance. Having the "image" or "likeness" of God means, in the simplest terms, that we were made to resemble God. Adam did not resemble God in the sense of God having flesh and blood. Scripture says that "God is a Spirit" **(John 4:24)** and therefore exists without a body. However, Adam's body did mirror the life of God insofar as it was created in perfect health and was not subject to death at the time when God formed him from the dust of the earth.

The image of God refers to the immaterial part of man. It sets man apart from the animal world, fits him for the dominion God intended him to have over the earth **(Genesis 1:28),** and enables him to commune with his Maker. It is a likeness mentally, morally, and socially.

The question then may be asked is what Is or who is God? God is a Spirit. He is a personal being without flesh and blood and therefore invisible. God is the Almighty. He is the Creator of the world. He is unlike any other gods. He is alive and is Holy. The Supreme Being with all infinite wisdom. He is the Omnipotent, Omnipresent, and Omniscience. God is Eternal. God is love.

Therefore, in order for us to have a better understanding of man we need to look at some of God's characteristics. The fact that the Bible tells us that God is a Spirit and that those that worship Him must worship Him in spirit and truth tells us that man has a spirit and is therefore a spiritual being. It is with man's spirit that he connects with and fellowship with God. Because man is a spiritual being he has the ability to interact with the spiritual realm whether good or evil.

God is love tells us that God is an emotional being. Therefore, man is an emotional being as well. Being emotional, man can feel pain, joy, sadness, love, hate etc. Man has the ability to forgive or don't forgive.

God is creative and according to Genesis God created the world by speaking. **Genesis 1: 3** states, *Then God said, "Let there be light"; and there was light.* Everything in creation God spoke into being and so it was with the exception of man. We are told that God formed man from the dust. It is then to be understood that man has the spiritual capability to create things in the spirit realm with his tongue.

Proverbs 18:20-21 [20] *A man's belly shall be satisfied with the fruit of his mouth; and with the increase of his lips shall he be filled.* [21] *Death and life are in the power of the tongue: and they that love it shall eat the fruit thereof.* **Job 22: 28** *You will also declare a thing, and it will be established for you; So, light will shine on your ways.* According to these two passages of scripture man's destiny lies in his tongue. We create our world by the way we speak. If we speak negatively our environment will be negative. If we speak positively, our environment will be positive. Adam demonstrated his God-given ability to be creative when he named the animals. Whatever Adam called them back at the beginning that's what they remain to be called to this day. It is established therefore that man's origin is from God and puts to bed the false theory of evolution that man evolved from monkeys.

Evolution teaches that man is nothing more than a highly developed animal. Man is nothing more than body, brain, bones, and blood. Evolution teaches that man has gradually evolved from lower animals (such as ape-like creatures) in a slowly changing process that has taken millions of years. Thus, the evolutionists would say that man is nothing more than a highly intelligent animal. They teach that man is very similar to the gorilla, except that man is smarter!

Evolution contradicts itself because the first cell that they state human life came from must have started somewhere. This somewhere, is creation that they deny existed. Evolution is nothing but a lie being told and sadly many fall for it.

Man is a child of God. Man is God's marvellous creation. Through his mind he can leap oceans, break through walls, and transcend the categories of time and space'.

Man has 'rational capacity; he has the unique ability to have fellowship with God. Man is a being of body, soul, and spirit. Some may argue that the passage in **Psalm 8** is stating that man is "a little god." However, I disagree with this contradictory statement because we were commanded in the book of Exodus not to have any other gods beside God. Therefore, why would God make man as a god? A god is an object or deity that is worshipped other than the true and living God. So why would God contradict Himself? The idea of man seeing himself as a god can be found in the book of **Genesis 3:5** For God doth know that in the day ye eat thereof, then your eyes shall be opened, and ye shall be as gods (God), knowing good and evil. This was a lie being told to mankind from the beginning by Satan. God would have already told man from the time He created him that he was made in his image and likeness. This is totally different from what Satan was saying about you shall be as gods. Satan has always harboured thoughts of being like God. **Isaiah 14:13-14.** *¹³ For thou hast said in thine heart, I will ascend into heaven, I will exalt my throne above the stars of God: I will sit also upon the mount of the congregation, in the sides of the north: ¹⁴ I will ascend above the heights of the clouds; I will be like the most High.*

When he said he wanted to be like the Most High he was simply saying he wanted to be worshipped (be a god). This is rather blasphemous and therefore theologians must be careful when they say they are interpreting the Bible and refer to mankind as a god. Lucifer was the archangel responsible for worship in Heaven. However, pride filled him up and he now wanted to be worshipped. The focus was now about him (I) rather than God. Man being made in God's image and likeness reflects God. It shows God working through man while God still gets the glory, worship and adoration that is due to His Holy Name.

Trichotomy Man vs Dichotomy Man

The word trichotomy refers to man in three dimensions as having a body, soul, and spirit. While dichotomy refers to man in two dimensions as having a body and soul or body and spirit. It should be made clear that dichotomist view the soul and spirit as the same entity which cannot be separated. However, my view according to Scripture is that God's word is able to separate the soul and the spirit.

Genesis 2:7 *states "And the Lord God formed man of the dust of the ground and breathed into his nostrils the breath of life; and man became a living being (soul)."*

This is a very loaded scripture with so much food for thought. Where it is stated, and the Lord God formed man this is referring to man's physical body formed from the clay. Breathed into his nostrils the breath of life is referring to God breathing spirit into man. Man becoming a living being is referring to man becoming a living soul. Therefore, in essence human beings could also be referred to as human souls. Therefore, from **Genesis 2:7** we can conclude that man is made up of a body, soul, and spirit. On the other hand, the dichotomist uses this verse to substantiate their theory that man is simply a body and a soul or a body and a spirit.

Genesis 1:26-27, [26] *And God said, let us make man in our image, after our likeness: and let them have dominion over the fish of the sea, and over the fowl of the air, and over the cattle, and over all the earth, and over every creeping thing that creep upon the earth.* [27] *So God created man in his own image, in the image of God created he him; male and female created he them.* In this passage we realise that there are similarities between God and man. Since man is made in the image and likeness of God, to understand the make-up of man we need to understand the make-up of God. According to **St John 4** we are told that God is a Spirit and they that worship him must worship Him in spirit and truth. **1 John 5:7** states, *for there are three that bear witness in heaven: The Father, the Word, and the Holy Spirit; and these three are one.*

It can be deduced from these passages that even though God is one He manifests Himself differently in different Eras. He was the Father in Creation, Son (Living Word) In Redemption and the Holy Spirit in the Church. However, throughout all the generation He remained as the One true God and not three Gods. When we go to Heaven, we will not see three separate thrones with three Gods but one throne with the Most High God sitting on it, enthroned with worshipping angels and Elders.

Man, therefore being made in God's image is one person but has three different entities as body, soul and spirit. Man made in the image and likeness of God has different applications and one of them applies to this subject the trichotomy of man. Man is referred to as tripartite which means there are three different entities to the one man.

Dichotomists argue that the spirit of man and the soul of man are inseparable. However, there are numerous scriptures that refute this point. **Hebrews 4:12** states, For the word of God is living and powerful, and sharper than any two-edged sword, piercing even to the division of soul and spirit, and of joints and marrow, and is a discerner of the thoughts and intents of the heart. Here we see in Hebrews 4 that the soul and spirit are separable. What can also be said from this passage is that the soul and spirit are tightly knitted. Even though tightly knitted they have different functions.

It should be noted in this connection that the Hebrew word for spirit is neshamah which means "wind," and the Hebrew word for soul is nephesh which means a "living (thinking) being." They are two totally different words and mean two totally different things. In addition, the Greek word for spirit is pneuma which means "breeze," and the Greek word for soul is psuche, which - like the Hebrew word, nephesh - means a "living (thinking) being." Again, they are two totally different words, and mean two totally different things. In addition, the Hebrew word for spirit, neshamah ("wind"), corresponds to the Greek word for spirit, pneuma ("breeze"), while the Hebrew word for soul, nephesh ("living (thinking) being") corresponds to the Greek word, psuche (also "living (thinking) being").

There are numerous other scriptures that represent man as a tripartite being. **1 Thessalonian 5:23** states, *now may the God of peace Himself sanctify you completely; and may your whole spirit, soul, and body be preserved blameless at the coming of our Lord Jesus Christ.* This verse clearly distinguished that a man is made up of body, soul, and spirit.

Man is made up of physical material, the body, that can be seen and touched. But he is also made up of immaterial aspects, which are intangible—this includes the soul and the spirit. These immaterial characteristics exist beyond the physical lifespan of the human body and are therefore eternal.

Man's threefold nature is this; spirit (the dimension of man which deals with the spiritual realm. The part of man that knows God. The soul is the dimension of man which deals with the mental realm. Man's intellect. The sensibilities and will. The part that reasons and thinks. The body is the dimension of man which deals with the physical realm. The house in which we live.

The Body

This is the entire material or physical structure of a human being—it is the physical part of a person. In the book of Romans, the author again connects the body, the mind (soul) and the spirit. *Therefore, I urge you, brethren, by the mercies of God, to present your **bodies** a living and holy sacrifice, acceptable to God, which is your reasonable (**spiritual**) service of worship. And do not be conformed to this world, but be transformed by the renewing of your **mind**, so that you may prove what the will of God is, that which is good and acceptable and perfect* (**Romans 12:1-2 NASB**). *For you have been bought with a price: therefore, glorify God in your **body*** (**1 Cor. 6:20**). "The body as our external part is the outer organ, possessing world-consciousness, that we may contact the material world. The body contains the soul, and the soul is the vessel that contains the spirit." Our body exists in and contacts the tangible things of the material world using our five physical senses. The body is the visible, external part of our being, and it contains the soul. Our soul is the vessel containing our spirit.

The Soul

Genesis 2:7 states that Man was created as a **"living soul."** The soul consists of the mind (which includes the conscience), the will and the emotions. The soul and the spirit are mysteriously tied together and make up what the Scriptures call the «heart.»

Proverbs 4:23 states *that we guard (watch over) our heart with all diligence because out of it flows (springs) the issues of life.* This shows that the "heart" is central to our emotions and will.

1 Corinthians 2:14 [14] *But the natural (psuchikos- soulish) man receives not the things of the Spirit of God: for they are foolishness unto him: neither can he know them, because they are spiritually discerned.*

"The soul is our very self (**Matt. 16:26; Luke 9:25**), a medium between our spirit and our body, possessing self-consciousness, that we may have our personality. "Our soul perceives things in the psychological realm. In fact, in Greek—the original language of the New Testament—the word for soul is psuche, which is also the root word of psychology. Our soul is our personality, who we are. With our soul we think, reason, consider, remember, and wonder. We experience emotions like happiness, love, sorrow, anger, relief, and compassion. And we're able to resolve, choose, and make decisions.

The Spirit

The spirit as our inmost part is the inner organ, possessing God-consciousness, that we may contact God (**John 4:24** [24] *God is a Spirit: and they that worship him must worship him in spirit and in truth.*; **Rom. 1:9** [9] *For God is my witness, whom I serve with my spirit in the gospel of his Son, that without ceasing I make mention of you always in my prayers;*).″

Man Was Made In God's Image And Likeness 25

The human spirit is the deepest part of a person. By means of this innermost part, we can contact God in the spiritual realm. No other creature was created by God with this third part.

In **Numbers 16:22**, Moses and Aaron, "... fell upon their faces and said, 'O God, God of **the spirits** of all **flesh**, when one-man sins, will you be angry with the entire congregation?'" This verse names God as the God of the **spirits** that are possessed by all humanity. Notice also that it mentions the **flesh (body)** of all mankind, connecting it with the spirit.

Hebrews 4:12 describes the separation between soul and spirit. For the word of God is living and active and sharper than any two-edged sword and piercing as far as **the division of soul and spirit**, of both joints and marrow, and able to judge the thoughts and intentions of the heart (**Heb. 4:12 NASB**). We see in this passage of Scripture that the soul and spirit can be divided—and that it is the Word of God that pierces our heart to bring the division of soul and spirit, something that only God can do.

The spirit of man is linked with the heart (the seat of our emotions) in some literature while the soul is linked with the mind. The Apostle Paul tells us in the book of Corinthians that our bodies are the Temple of the Holy Spirit. Before the fall of man, his spirit was in tuned to the Holy Spirit (awareness of God's presence). Unless an individual has his spirit regenerated by accepting Jesus Christ as Lord and Saviour, through water baptism, according to **Acts 2:38** and **John 3:5** that person's spirit will be drawn to do the works of the flesh and connects to the Kingdom of darkness. In the book of **Psalm 51:10** we see where David prayed to God not to cast him away from His presence also for God to renew a right spirit within him. This is the same David who in **Psalm 23:3** states He restores my soul. So, it is clear that outside of God's presence man's spirit can become wrong. However, in God's presence man's soul can be restored. As stated above the soul speaks of our mind, will and intellect. Different circumstances in life can affect a person's mind resulting in mental illness. However, God can restore that sick soul (mental illness).

Understanding Who We Are

When an individual fully understands their make up as a human being they will approach life with utmost respect for God. The fact that we were made in the image and likeness of God will enable us to realise we are not a normal being. We are far more valuable to God than the animals of the field.

I remember years ago, living in London. One Sunday afternoon, a little boy called Theo, about six years old, and his Mom were visiting my aunty Daphne and her family. Theo was playing computer games at the time with my cousin Tre who was about the same age as Theo. Something went wrong while the two boys were playing, and Theo got upset. He started screaming and became angry. My aunty Daphne said to him, "are you an animal why are you behaving in that manner?" Theo replied, "we are all animals!" This, to the amazement of my aunty, myself and the other adults who were present at the time. A six-year-old boy has had it drilled into him that humans are animals. Hence, he didn't mind behaving in a manner that reflects the behaviour of an animal.

Evolutionists wrongfully teach that we evolved from apes. This is what the father of lies wants us to believe, that we came from and are animals. Animals don't have a spirit to communicate with God and neither do they have a soul that will be judged after death. God made mankind uniquely. When he created Adam, He gave him authority over all the animals. Through our spirit we can connect with God, as our souls hope in Him. Recognising that our bodies are worth more to God than any multi-million-pound building. No finely designed cathedral can be compared to our bodies in God's sight, seeing that our bodies are the temple of the Holy Ghost. If we know our true worth we will present our bodies as a living sacrifice, holy and acceptable unto God which is our reasonable service. We will not be conformed to this world but instead we will be transformed by the renewing of our minds.

Spiritual Authority Given to Adam At Creation

At creation, Adam was given authority to have dominion over the earth, seen in how he named all the living creatures **(Genesis 1:27-30; 2:19-20).** Having God's authority meant Adam was beneath God's authority, and in subjection to Him. A hedge of protection was round about Adam and his wife. At the onset of creation, they had dominion collectively, or so it appears. It also appears that Adam had a greater degree of responsibility, having been created first, and having been given the first commandment (not to partake of the forbidden tree).

Genesis 1:26-28 [26] *And God said, let us make man in our image, after our likeness: and let them have dominion over the fish of the sea, and over the fowl of the air, and over the cattle, and over all the earth, and over every creeping thing that creeps upon the earth . . .*

This dominion or authority in **Genesis 1** was three-dimensional, in the waters, in the air and on the land. That means when God created man, His intention was for man to take control of his environment. He did not create Adam and then appoint him as His manager. He created Adam to rule–a living, speaking spirit, like his Creator. It is man's nature to rule just as it is God's nature to rule. God's delegated authority was conferred on man as God's under-ruler.

Psalm 8:3-8 [3] *When I consider thy heavens, the work of thy fingers, the moon and the stars, which thou hast ordained;* [4] *What is man, that thou art mindful of him? and the son of man, that thou visit him?* [5] *For thou hast made him a little lower than the angels, and hast crowned him with glory and honour.* [6] *Thou made him to have dominion over the works of thy hands; thou hast put all things under his feet:* [7] *All sheep and oxen, yea, and the beasts of the field;* [8] *The fowl of the air, and the fish of the sea, and whatsoever passes through the paths of the seas.* Here in the book of **Psalm 8** we see a confirmation of the three-dimensional authority that God gave to man when He created him in Genesis. God gave Adam His own authority over everything on this planet and crowned him with His glory **(Psalm 8:4-5).** Man was not only crowned with glory and honour but was made a little lower than the angels. We are *"lower than the angels"* in that we are mortal, subject to physical death. However, the good news is that, once we are resurrected with glorified bodies, we will be *"equal unto the angels,"* meaning that we will never experience physical death again. **Luke 20:34-36** [34] *And Jesus answering said unto them, The children of this world marry, and are given in marriage:* [35] *But they which shall be accounted worthy to obtain that world, and the resurrection from the dead, neither marry, nor are given in marriage:* [36] *Neither can they die any more: for they are equal unto the angels; and are the children of God, being the children of the resurrection.*

CHAPTER 2
The Fall Of Man

The fall of man, or the fall, is a term used in Christian mythology to describe the transition of the first man and woman from a state of innocent obedience to God to a state of guilty disobedience. The word fall would bring to mind a condition of an object that was standing vertically now lays horizontal. One definition of the word fall is "to come or go down quickly from a high place or position.

Man being a fallen creature speaks about Adam and Eve being in right standing with God and because of sin (disobedience) they are now out of position. Out of position refers to man operating not as God originally intended for him. When God created man, they were living in peace and harmony with God. Scriptures tells us in Genesis that God used to come down in the cool of the day and have fellowship with man. How pleasant and wonderful that must have been. The Almighty God leaving His throne in Heaven to come to Earth in the Garden of Eden where man lives to fellowship with him.

The thoughts that come to mind are what were some of the conversations God would exchange with man then and visa-versa? Was it a time of worship in the Garden of Eden? I can imagine Adam and Eve singing praises to the Almighty God. I say this because human beings are created with the innate desire to worship. It must be this harmonious atmosphere between God and man that would arouse jealousy in Satan to tempt man to sin resulting in him not being able to share in this awesome moment with his Creator on a daily basis. Scripture tells us in the books of Ezekiel and Isaiah that it was Lucifer who used to give worship to God. However, he lost this privilege when he became filled with pride and wanted to take the worship for himself. This resulted in him being kicked out of Heaven along with a third of the angels. From a position of having access to everything that was good in the Garden of Eden at will, man through disobedience to God's command not to eat of the tree of knowledge and evil found himself on the outskirts of the Garden of Eden suddenly.

Disobedience to God's Word

Genesis 2:15-17 [15] *And the Lord God took the man and put him into the garden of Eden to dress it and to keep it.* [16] *And the Lord God commanded the man, saying, of every tree of the garden thou mayest freely eat:* [17] *But of the tree of the knowledge of good and evil, thou shalt not eat of it: for in the day that thou eat thereof thou shalt surely die.* In the book of **John 1** the Bible declares that In the beginning was the Word, and the Word was with God and the Word was

God. This lets us know that God is His Word. Therefore, when we disobey God's Word, we are in fact disobeying God. There are rewards when we obey God's Word and on the other hand there are grave consequences for disobeying them. **Proverbs 13:13** [13] *Whosoever despises the word shall be destroyed: but he that fears (reverence, honour, obey) the commandment shall be rewarded.*

This is God's principle and that's how He has established it from the beginning. I mentioned above that God's Word is who He is. When I was growing up as a young man in Jamaica, they had this saying "a man's word makes him a man and your word is your bond." **Psalm 138:2** [2] *I will worship toward thy holy temple and praise thy name for thy lovingkindness and for thy truth: for thou hast magnified thy word above all thy name.* In Scripture we know God's Name is Powerful. In the Old Testament One of God's most significant Name was Jehovah. While in the New Testament the Name that God is revealed by is Jesus. Scriptures goes on to say in **Philippians 2:9-10** [9] *Wherefore God also hath highly exalted him, and given him a name which is above every name:* [10] *That at the name of Jesus every knee should bow, of things in heaven, and things in earth, and things under the earth.*

The Name signifies authority, but God's Word is who He is. Hence the reason He has magnified his word above His Name. Therefore, when we disobey God's Word or commands we sin.

In **Genesis 2** God clearly commanded the man what trees he could eat from and the one he shouldn't eat from.

It is clear this command was given to Adam and not Eve. However, being the head of the marriage and getting such serious command it would have been expected Adam would have instructed Eve regarding the same. In **Genesis 3** we see how Satan twisted God's Word and deceived Eve, who in turn was able to influence her husband to do the same.

Genesis 3:1,11-14 *Now the serpent was more subtil (crafty) than any beast of the field which the Lord God had made. And he said unto the woman, Yea, hath God said, Ye shall not eat of every tree of the garden?* [11] *And He said, who told thee that thou was naked? Has thou eaten of the tree, whereof I commanded thee that thou shouldest not eat?* [12] *And the man said, the woman whom thou gave to be with me, she gave me of the tree, and I did eat . . .* Disobeying God's Word resulted in a chain reaction of blame game. God rightly went to Adam first because He put him in charge and it was to Adam God gave the command. Husbands, God has put us in charge of our families and he expects us to lead our families as He God has commanded us to. It doesn't matter what's happening around us, who is disobeying God's Word etc. God expects us as the head and leaders of our families to stand and obey His commands.

Eve was backed in a corner by herself and became vulnerable to be tempted by the serpent. Wives God has created your husbands to be your covering. Be careful how you go about doing things without the knowledge of your husband. The enemy will seek to use this opportunity to lead you in a vulnerable position that could spell trouble for you and your family. Both Adam and Eve were held responsible for disobeying God's command. However, God saw Adam as the main perpetrator.

Romans 5:12-14: *12 Therefore, just as through one man sin entered the world, and death through sin, and thus death spread to all men, because all sinned— 13 (For until the law sin was in the world, but sin is not imputed when there is no law. 14 Nevertheless death reigned from Adam to Moses, even over those who had not sinned according to the likeness of the transgression of Adam, who is a type of Him who was to come.* Through Adam's disobedience, the entire human race was plunged into sin and a separation from God's presence. This disobedience brought spiritual death, physical death, sickness and disease to mankind. He also lost the privilege to worship God in spirit and truth on a daily basis as he used to do at will. Even though the generations after Adam and Eve didn't physically eat the forbidden fruit the consequences of Adam's disobedience apply to us today. King David understood this and wrote in **Psalm 51:5** Behold, I was brought forth in iniquity, and in sin my mother conceived me.

The consequence of Adam's disobedience means sin is a contaminate disease that will infect every human being born upon this earth. One of the effects of this contamination of sin is that man has an unmissable appointment with death. Scripture tells us that it is appointed unto man to die once but after that judgement. With this said man is like an accident waiting to happen as death is inevitable. Death is the ultimate consequence of mankind falling. As mentioned above there are two types of death that was as a result of this fall.

As soon as they sinned, Adam and Eve instantly experienced spiritual death, that status where, because of our sin and unrighteousness, we are accounted dead by a righteous and Holy God who can in His perfection no longer have any direct contact with us (except on His own grace terms of salvation through our acceptance on a non-meritorious faith basis of Christ's saving work on the cross).

Examining the quote above we would conclude that spiritual death is to be excluded from the presence of God. It is where it is impossible for man to communicate with God directly except through the redemptive work of Jesus Christ. The presence of God mentioned here is not the omnipresence of God which speaks about God being present everywhere at once. Instead it is dealing with man not having direct contact with the Holy Spirit of God. As a result, man's spirit cannot make a link with God's Spirit. This results in spiritual malnutrition. In the book of Acts we are reminded that it is in Him (Jesus Christ) we live, move and have our being (existence). That means outside of God we are dead spiritually. This was the state Adam and Eve found themselves in.

Their bodies were also instantly rendered mortal. The process of decay and degeneration began immediately upon partaking of the fruit. Under the conditions that pertained in this antediluvian (ancient, primitive) world, Adam and Eve and many of their children had, by our standards, exceptionally long lives, but even living a thousand years seems insignificant when compared to immortality. Eating the forbidden fruit contrary to the explicit prohibition of the Lord God also eventually destroyed their bodies (physical death). Even the restoration of their relationship with God through their faith in His promised Messiah would not erase this appointment with physical death **(Heb.9:27).**

God when he made man, built in man the immortal trait. However, as a result of the fall of mankind their bodies are now mortal. Whereas man at the beginning of time would live to become over 900 years old, mortality steps in and rapidly reduces that life span to about 70 years old. According to **Psalm 90:10** we are told that the years of a man are 70 and by reason of strength they may be 80 years old. Compare this to Methuselah in **Genesis 5** who was the oldest man to ever lived at the grand age of 969 years old. Other punishments as a result of the fall of man are man eating bread by the sweat of his brow that is by hard work. It was also meted out that the woman would give birth in pain according to the book of Genesis.

We Are Tempted By Our Own Lusts

The word temptation means to be enticed by evil. No human being is above being tempted. The Apostle Paul summarises it this way, "when I want to do good, evil presents itself or evil is present." Evil is present around us and is an uninvited guest that doesn't know protocols and seeks to gate crash every opportunity it gets in our lives.

King David, in the Book of **2 Samuels 11**, was meant to be at war. However, he absconded from his kingly duty of leading his people into war. Evil presented itself to him as Bathsheba was washing herself. The evil wasn't Bathsheba but the acts that David did. These acts included adultery, murder, stealing and lying. It is said that the Devil provides work for idle hands. Whenever we are not doing the things we are called to do or we step out of God's will, we leave ourselves vulnerable to be tempted. Heeding to these temptations can be our downfall and not just ours but it can impact our family members for generations.

In the book of James 1 we are told that it's a blessing when we endure (go through) temptation. The temptations are a part of our daily walk as children of God. The blessing in enduring temptations is that we will receive a crown of life when this life is ended. This is a sure promise from God for us to look forward to if we love Him. It is our love for God that's going to enable us in the time of temptation to make a righteous stand. Even if everyone else around us is falling for it. Even when we are mocked, scorned, ridiculed and called all manner of names. A reminder of one of the great commandments, **Mark 12:29-30** [29] And Jesus answered him, the first of all the commandments is, Hear, O Israel; The Lord our God is one Lord: [30] And thou shalt love the Lord thy God with all thy heart, and with all thy soul, and with all thy mind, and with all thy strength: this is the first commandment.

God expects us as His children to love Him with our entire being. That is, presenting ourselves daily as a living sacrifice, holy and acceptable to Him. That we should not be conformed to this world but be transformed by the renewing of our minds. It is God's Word that is going to renew our minds and bring the transformation that He desires in us.

James 2 goes on to say we shouldn't blame God when we are tempted and say I am tempted by God. God cannot be tempted with evil and neither tempts He any man. But every man is tempted when we are drawn away from his own lust and enticed. Many people are quick to blame God for when situations go wrong in their lives. However, if we truly examine ourselves and the root cause of our problems, we would realise it was our own lust that drew us into our temptations. We then fail to overcome our temptations and start to sin against God. Then according to Scripture, sin when it is conceived, brings forth death.

God is such a loving God. Even when we have failed Him and deserved to die, He still extends His love and His grace towards us. For some of us He gives us chances beyond chances. Let us not be ungrateful today and start a blame game with God for our shortcomings in life. Instead let us draw closer to God by first repenting of our errors, start counting our blessings one by one and it may surprise us to see how much God has done in our lives. I love what the Scripture says, God cannot be tempted by evil and neither tempts He any man. We need to remember the God we serve is the Holy one of Israel, Holiness is His nature. This God (Jesus Christ) is the Light of the World and there is no darkness in Him. God doesn't desire any bad things for anyone but instead thoughts that are good and not evil to lead us to an expected end.

Lust is a strong desire to do something or an immensely powerful feeling of wanting something. It's not just about something sexual. Lust is like a craving. This is what entices us and leads us into being tempted. Our fleshly (sin nature) man will always have the ability to be drawn into temptation by our lust. That's why if we are going to prove our love for God and live for Him, we must walk in the Spirit and not in the flesh. This where our desires must be subjected to what God desires and our will have to be subjected to the will of God. The flesh must come under subjection of the leading of the Holy Spirit. This is putting the saying dying daily to ourselves into practice.

James 1:12-15 [12] *Blessed is the man that endures temptation: for when he is tried, he shall receive the crown of life, which the Lord hath promised to them that love him.* [13] *Let no man say when he is tempted, I am tempted of God: for God cannot be tempted with evil, neither tempts he any man:* [14] *But every man is tempted, when he is drawn away of his own lust, and enticed.* [15] *Then when lust hath conceived, it bringeth forth sin: and sin, when it is finished, bringeth forth death.*

Genesis 3:1-5 *Now the serpent was more subtil than any beast of the field which the Lord God had made. And he said unto the woman, Yea, hath God said, Ye shall not eat of every tree of the garden?* [2] *And the woman said unto the serpent, we may eat of the fruit of the trees of the garden:* [3] *But of the fruit of the tree which is in the midst of the garden, God*

The Fall Of Man

hath said, Ye shall not eat of it, neither shall ye touch it, lest ye die . . .

In the above Scripture in **Genesis 3** we are told the Serpent (Satan came in the form of a serpent) was more subtil (cunning) than any beast of the field. From the physical eyes we would say oh this is a beautiful creature, and it doesn't mean us any harm. However, it is the spirit that is behind it, the spirit that is behind the person. Satan disguised himself as a beautiful, cunning and harmless serpent. He had one intention and that was to get Adam and Eve to doubt and eventually disobey God's Word. That was not his ultimate aim but instead he came to steal, kill and destroy them. That's right he came to rob them of the dominion and Spiritual authority God gave them. He came to kill them knowing on the day they ate of the tree of knowledge of good and evil they would surely die. He came eventually to destroy them, that is, when Satan is through with us our soul is lost in eternal damnation.

Just as Satan disguised himself as a beautiful, harmless serpent in Genesis. This is what he, his ministers and agents practice. **2 Corinthians 11:13-15** [13] *For such are false apostles, deceitful workers, transforming themselves into the apostles of Christ.* [14] *And no marvel; for Satan himself is transformed into an angel of light.* [15] *Therefore it is no great thing if his ministers also be transformed as the ministers of righteousness; whose end shall be according to their works.*

Deception is one of the biggest weapons of Satan. It is through deception he will get us to disobey God's Word and through deception Satan and his agents will present as

Ministers of righteousness. That's why it is important for us to try the spirit operating behind people and for us to pray for the gift of the discerning of spirits. Sad to say there are many ministers of Satan who present to be ministers of Christ operating in a lot of church organisations. Some of these so-called church organisations are very big while some are small. Now we understand why the Scripture says in **Ephesians chapter 6** that we wrestle not against flesh and blood but against principalities, against powers, against the rulers of the darkness of this world, against spiritual wickedness in high places.

Just as Satan disguised himself and presented as a beautiful, harmless serpent to Eve with the intent to ultimately destroy her and her husband. We need to be mindful that there are people under the influence of deceptive and unclean spirits. They will present as being kind and loving to us initially, some of them are always smiling. They have one intention and that is to see our downfall. However, we must be wise as a serpent and harmless as a dove.

Eve was the most vulnerable between her and Adam. The Bible called her the weaker vessel **(1 Peter 3:7).** Satan knew she was more vulnerable than her husband. He therefore sought after her to tempt her. **1 Peter 5:8** Be sober, be vigilant; because your adversary the devil, as a roaring lion, walketh about, seeking whom he may devour: Whether Satan presents himself as a serpent, a lion or as a dragon, he will always seek out the vulnerable (those whom he may devour). That's why we need to be spiritually alert. We also need to come under the blood-stained banner of Jesus Christ and not leave ourselves uncovered. **Psalm 91:1-3** *He that* dwells in the secret place of the Most High shall abide under the shadow of the Almighty. ² *I will say of the Lord, He is my refuge and my fortress: my God; in him will I trust.* ³ *Surely, he shall deliver thee from the snare of the fowler, and from the noisome pestilence.*

Let us hold fast to God's word no matter what circumstances we are going through. **Psalm 119:89** Forever oh Lord thy word is settled in Heaven. God's Word is eternal and is unchangeable. However, Satan will always seek to bring us to a place for us to doubt God's Word and to think it's untrue. He was successful in doing that to Eve in Genesis 3. He twisted God's Word and presented God as a liar. This eventually sowed doubt in Eve's mind and she fell for the temptation. She was eventually drawn away from the truth of God's Word by her own lust.

God told Adam and Eve on the day you eat of the tree of knowledge of good and evil you will surely die. Satan came along and twisted the truth and said you will not surely die. We need to be careful who we take council from after God has clearly spoken to us. God clearly spoke through prophecy concerning His perfect will for our lives. However, there are some heave droppers who are dream killers, operating under the guise of the Devil. **Psalm 1:1** *Blessed is the man who walks not in the council of the ungodly, nor stands in the way of sinners . . .* Who are we as the children of God taking counsel from as it relates to God's will concerning our lives.

Satan has partial access to the prophecies God has spoken concerning us and his aim is to bring us to a place to abort those prophecies. I decree that we will get to a place and hold fast to the truth of God's Word no matter how much lies the adversary tells us. Even when God leads us through the fiery furnace His Word remains true. Take responsibility for the prophecies that have been genuinely spoken from the Throne of Grace concerning your life. Hold fast to what God has said if you fail to do that you'll eventually be aborting the prophecies and your dreams because you fell to the temptations of the lies of Satan.

Genesis 3:5-7 [5] For God doth know that in the day ye eat thereof, then your eyes shall be opened, and ye shall be as gods, knowing good and evil. [6] And when the woman saw that the tree was good for food, and that it was pleasant to the eyes, and a tree to be desired to make one wise, she took of the fruit thereof, and did eat, and gave also unto her husband with her; and he did eat. [7] And the eyes of them both were opened, and they knew that they were naked; and they sewed fig leaves together and made themselves aprons.

1 John 2:15-17 [15] *Love not the world, neither the things that are in the world. If any man loves the world, the love of the Father is not in him.* [16] *For all that is in the world, the lust of the flesh, and the lust of the eyes, and the pride of life, is not of the Father, but is of the world.* [17] *And the world passes away, and the lust thereof: but he that doeth the will of God abides forever.*

Lust of The Flesh

Mankind was tempted in three main areas in the Garden of Eden. Satan uses these areas to trap mankind. I remember my late Bishop Neville Hamilton from Ewarton Gospel Lighthouse Church in Jamaica. He normally gives us wise counsels. As young men he usually said to us to be careful of the three G's. That was the girls (lust of the flesh), the gold (lust of the eyes) and the glory (pride of life).

According to the above passages the first area of temptation was the lust of the flesh. **Genesis 3:6** *And when the woman saw that the tree was good for food (lust of the flesh)...* **1 John 2:16** *For all that is in the world, the lust of the flesh...*

The lust of the flesh is everything that appeals to the sensual (carnal) and natural appetite. Although natural body desires are not innately evil (e.g., the need for food and drink.) etc the devil can use these legitimate desires (legitimate within their own limits) to enslave man. In this type of temptation, Satan uses inner licit desires to produce illicit carnal passions (for example, gluttony, fornication). The children of Israel capitulated under this type of sin when "the people sat down to eat and drink and rose up to play" **(1 Corinthians 10:7; Exodus 32:6).** The devil tried to tempt Jesus by the lust of the flesh when he urged him to turn stones into bread **(Matthew 4:3).**

In most cases the word "lust" is used with a negative connotation in some New Testament passages e.g. *"But put on the Lord Jesus Christ, and make no provision for the flesh, to fulfil its lusts"* **(Rom. 13:14).** *"I say then: Walk in the Spirit, and you shall not fulfil the lust of the flesh"* **(Gal. 5:16).** *"For when they speak great swelling words of emptiness, they allure through the lusts of the flesh, through lewdness, the ones who* *have actually escaped from those who live in error"* **(2 Pet. 2:18)**.

The "lust of the flesh" then is an evil desire for the things of the flesh. The first thing that usually comes to mind is adultery and fornication. "Adultery" is usually used in the Bible to describe all illicit sexual relations between one or more married individuals. "Fornication" is a rather broad term used to describe any illicit sexual conduct, including pre-marital sex or even homosexuality. Adultery and fornication are both "works of the flesh" **(Gal. 5:19)**, and as such will keep those guilty out of heaven.

God designed marriage to keep people from sexual sins **(1 Cor. 7:1-5)**. The marital bed is holy. The Hebrew writer tells us that "Marriage is honourable among all, and the bed undefiled; but fornicators and adulterers God will judge" **(Heb. 13:4)**. This marital union is so sacred that God has only allowed one reason for a person to divorce their spouse and marry another, i.e., sexual immorality. Jesus plainly said, "whoever divorces his wife, except for sexual immorality, and marries another, commits adultery; and whoever marries her who is divorced commits adultery" **(Matt. 19:9)**.

Lust of The Eyes

The lust of the eyes is everything that appeals to the eye's unquenchable demands **(Ecclesiastes 1:8)**. In this type of temptation, Satan uses external attraction (whether innately good, as a desire for a house or a car, or innately bad, as a desire for a neighbour's wife) to produce covetousness. Eve in Genesis and Achan **in Joshua** yielded to this type of sin when they coveted what was forbidden. Satan unsuccessfully tempted Jesus by the lust of the eyes when he "showed Him all the kingdoms of the world and their glory. And he said to Him, 'All these things I will give You if You will fall down and worship me'" **(Matthew 4:8-9).**

The "lust of the eyes" speaks of eyes that are delighted with riches and rich possessions; this is the lust of covetousness.

Those men whom Moses appointed as "rulers of thousands, rulers of hundreds, rulers of fifties, and rulers of tens" were to be "able men, such as fear God, men of truth, hating covetousness" **(Exod. 18:21)**.

The Ten Commandments included a warning against covetousness. *"You shall not covet your neighbour's house; you shall not covet your neighbour's wife, nor his male servant, nor his female servant, nor his ox, nor his donkey, nor anything that is your neighbour's"* **(Exod. 20:17)**. Solomon tells us *"he who hates covetousness will prolong his days"* **(Prov. 28:16)**. The Lord Jesus admonishes us to *"take heed and beware of covetousness, for one's life does not consist in the abundance of the things he possesses"* **(Luke 12:15)**. In **Colossians** Paul instructs us to "put to death your members which are on the earth: fornication, uncleanness, passion, evil desire, and covetousness, which is idolatry."

The Pride of Life

The pride of life is everything that appeals to conceit, egotism, and pride. In this type of temptation, the Devil can use the thought of personal achievements to produce a lawless self-sufficient attitude. If a person falls prey to the pride of life, there is no longer a battle against the flesh; Satan has won the sensual and intellectual battle. The children of Israel surrendered to this type of sin when they "acted proudly, hardened their necks, and did not heed to God's commandments" **(Nehemiah 9:16)**. The devil tried to tempt Jesus by the pride of life when he "took Him up into the holy city, set Him on the pinnacle of the temple", and urged Him to defy God **(Matthew 4:5-7)**.

The "pride of life" is a vain craving for honour and applause, or the stubborn mind-set that will not allow one to repent of and confess their sins. King Saul and the Pharisee were examples of Biblical characters who fell prey to the pride of life. Solomon instructs us Proverbs **8:13**, *"The fear of the Lord is to hate evil; pride and arrogance and the evil way and the perverse mouth I hate."* The Pharisee prayed as one who needed no forgiveness, and got none. The tax collector prayed as one who needed God's forgiveness, and he received it.

Pride oftentimes keeps Christians from truly repenting of their sins, especially when their sin is public in nature. Sometimes Christians refuse to repent of their sins because they are not aware of them—they do not think they are guilty. But let's be honest about the matter, most of the time an unrepentant heart does not come from lack of knowledge, but from foolish pride—they know they are guilty, but they won't admit to it. They will not admit their sin and then repent of it, and absurd pride is so often at the heart of the matter—they cannot stand before the ones whom they sinned against and say, "I have sinned."

The book of Proverbs covers a lot about selfish pride and destruction it brings. It reminds us that "when pride comes, then comes shame" **(Prov. 11:2)**, and "by pride comes nothing but strife" **(Prov. 13:10)**, and warns us that "pride goes before destruction, and a haughty spirit before a fall" **(Prov. 16:18)**.

The Temptation of Jesus Christ

Matthew 4: 1-11 Then Jesus *led the Spirit into the wilderness to be tempted by the devil. ² And when he had fasted forty days and forty nights, he was afterward an hungred. ³ And when the tempter came to him, he said, If thou be the Son of God, command that these stones be made bread.*

⁴But he answered and said, It is written, Man shall not live by bread alone, but by every word that proceeds out of the mouth of God . . . (Also **Luke 4:1-13**).

The above passages **in Matthew 4 and Luke 4** highlights the temptation of the Lord Jesus Christ who was God. That's right, when the Holy Spirit, who is God came upon the Virgin Mary and the power of the Highest overshadowed her, she was conceived with a "Holy Thing." Jesus Christ who was called the Son of God, was fully God (the Spirit that was in Him, for God is a Spirit . . .) and He was fully man (His body and soul). The full humanity of Christ is seen in that he experienced all human weaknesses and limitations of having a human body, mind, soul, and emotions; yet he was without sin **(Hebrews 4:15-16)**. So, in a nutshell in order to redeem mankind God who is a Spirit clothed Himself in a human body. This was the person of Jesus Christ who was fully God and fully man.

He was tempted in three areas as Adam and Eve. That is the lust of the flesh, the lust of the eyes and the pride of life. Yet he did not sin. **Hebrews 4:14-15** [14] *Seeing then that we have a great high priest, that is passed into the heavens, Jesus the Son of God, let us hold fast our profession.* [15] *For we have not an high priest which cannot be touched with the feeling of our infirmities; but was in all points tempted like as we are, yet without sin.*

It should be made clear in the temptation of Jesus Christ, that it was His humanity that was tempted and not His Divinity. **James 1:13-14** [13] *Let no man say when he is tempted, I am tempted of God: for God cannot be tempted with evil, neither tempts he any man:* [14] *But every man is tempted, when he is drawn away of his own lust, and enticed.* **Matthew 4:1** Then Jesus led the Spirit into the wilderness to be tempted by the devil. **Matthew chapter 4** is telling us that the Divinity in Jesus led his humanity into the wilderness to be tempted by the devil. Even though Jesus was led by the Spirit indwelling in Him, the temptation was done by the devil. This proves that Scripture is consistent. There are seasons of testing and trials that God would have us go through as His children. He would permit other nations to persecute Israel for the sole purpose of realigning them in His perfect will. God allowed Nebuchadnezzar to put the three Hebrew boys to the test in the fiery furnace.

God who is a Spirit, who was indwelling in the body of Jesus Christ and to identify with humanity, in order to bring about redemption for mankind, cannot be tempted with evil and neither tempts He any man. This then concludes that it was Jesus's humanity that was tempted in the areas of the lust of the flesh, lust of the eyes and the pride of life.

The devil tried to tempt Jesus by the lust of the flesh when he urged him to turn stones into bread **(Matthew 4:3)**. He knew Jesus was hungry because He was fasting for forty days. Therefore, His humanity would naturally desire food. Fasting is a time that we make up in our minds to consecrate ourselves to God for a specific period. In the process we sacrifice certain things including food in order that we bring the flesh under subjection of the Holy Spirit. Satan will always tempt us in the areas we have needs and are most vulnerable. We are drawn into temptation by our desires (lust). Had Jesus fell for the temptation, His Divine assignment to redeem mankind would not be accomplished because this Lamb of God who was slain before the foundation of the World had to be tempted in all points but didn't sin.

The devil tried to tempt Jesus by the lust of the eyes when he "showed Him all the kingdoms of the world and their glory. And he said to Him, 'All these things I will give You if You will fall down and worship me'" **(Matthew 4:8-9)**. Satan was able to tempt and deceive Adam and Eve in an area where they weren't certain who they were. They were made in the image and likeness of God. Satan was able to influence them if they eat of the tree of knowledge of good and evil they would "be like gods." The fact that they were made in God's image and likeness you thought that would be enough. It's the same trick he tried to pull on Jesus by offering Him the kingdoms of the world that He created. It is so important as a child of God we know who we are in Christ. If not, the devil will have us toss to and from with every wind of deceptive and lying doctrines.

When we look deeper into Satan telling Adam and Eve that if they disobey God's command they'll be like gods, it brings a parallel when he was in Heaven as an archangel of worship. **Isaiah 14:13-14** [13] *For thou hast said in thine heart, I will ascend into heaven, I will exalt my throne above the stars of God: I will sit also upon the mount of the congregation, in the sides of the north:* [14] *I will ascend above the heights of the clouds; I will be like the Most High.* From his time of being an archangel in Heaven, he desired to be like the Most High. Not only that, he wanted to go above God. That was the tune he sang to the ears of Eve, and this resulted in their downfall.

He offered Jesus the kingdoms of the world that He already created and owned. In exchange of Him bowing and down and offering him Satan worship. That's what he wanted from his time in Heaven, not to offer worship anymore as an archangel but instead to be worshipped. All because pride entered his heart. The sad reality is many people today are purposely disobeying God's command because they fell for the lie that they'll be like gods. Many have sold their souls in order to gain the riches of this world, by bowing down and offering worship to Satan. As in the days of king Nebuchadnezzar many people are bowing down and offering worship to many idols at the sound of the

The Fall Of Man

"music." Like the three Hebrew boys can we hold fast to our faith and refuse to bow to any foreign gods but only offer true worship to the only True and Living God, who is the Lord Jesus Christ. What music are we listening and dancing to as sons and daughters of our Heavenly Father? A lot of these musicians and singers have bowed their knees and have offered their worship to the foreign gods. Are we going to let our lives and the lives of our children be influenced and controlled by the sounds these idolatrous musicians and singers are producing? The Bible let us know that Satan is the prince of the air (airwave). Yes, he does influence most of what happens in the media (radio, television, internet, social media etc).

The devil tried to tempt Jesus by the pride of life when he "took Him up into the holy city, set Him on the pinnacle of the temple", and urged Him to defy God **(Matthew 4:5-7** by throwing himself down from the pinnacle of the temple in order to easily declare himself as the Messiah and prove that God was working for him.

By choosing to jump, Jesus would have been following His own will, not following in His Father's ways. It would have been an attempt to bolster Himself and not follow God's blueprint for what was to occur. Jesus would have been acting presumptuously.

Now, didn't the Father back up Jesus' ministry with many miracles? Jesus healed, Jesus drove out demons, and Jesus raised people from the dead. However, He did this with the Father's blessing. Read the account of Lazarus being raised from the dead when you get the chance, and you will see

Jesus praying out loud to the Father, rather than following His own will. Jesus, even in this case, performed the miracle in the manner, time and place that the Father determined.

The key point The Lord Jesus demonstrated when it comes on to overcoming temptation was to rightly divide and quote God's Word against Satan. Satan has knowledge of God's Word but as the father of all lies there is no truth in him. Therefore, he can't help but to twist God's Word and with that create lies. It's not how many years we've professed to being born again or our church titles that's going to enable us to overcome temptations. It is us as sons and daughters of God taking up the sword of the Spirit that is sharper than any two-edged sword and using it to counteract the lies of Satan each time he comes to tempt us.

Satan is very persistent and for 40 days he tempted and tested Jesus. It's the same with us, he is very persistent in all that he will throw at us in order for us to fall. However, what will determine if we fail or overcome is us doing like the Lord Jesus and reminding Satan that it is written "man shall not live by bread alone but by every word that proceeds out of God's mouth. Adam and Eve failed and fell because they had failed to hold fast to these principles. They allowed Satan to cast doubt in their minds as it related to the truth of God's Word and who they were. Where Adam and Eve failed, Jesus Christ overcame.

As the Redeemer He showed us that every temptation that we face is such as is common among men but for every temptation God Has made a way of escape. **1 Corinthians**

4:10 ¹³ *There hath no temptation taken you, but such as is common to man: but God is faithful, who will not suffer (allow) you to be tempted above that ye are able; but will with the temptation also make a way to escape, that ye may be able to bear it.* This passage lets us know that from the beginning the same temptations that Adam and Eve encountered, it's the same temptations that we'll also encounter. The temptations are common (lust of the flesh, lust of the eyes and the pride of life). One of the refreshing things about this passage is that it reminds us that in the heat of being tempted by the devil, God is faithful. God being faithful means that He is trustworthy.

Therefore, even though he allows us to be tempted, we can rest assured, He will not allow us to be tempted above that which we are able to bear (take on, tolerate). Not only that but He has made a "way" of escape to overcome every temptation. We need to remember that Jesus is the Way, the Truth and the Life. That is right, Jesus went ahead and showed us how to overcome temptations. That way of escape is being able to rightly divide God's word in the hour of temptation. Like the psalmist we must hide God's Word in our heart that we will not sin against Him **(Psalm 119: 11).**

God's Word is so powerful in that, not only does it divide between soul and spirit but with God's Word hidden in our hearts, we can discern every lie and every lying spirit. Jesus who is the "Way" of escape in overcoming temptations was also the Word. Each time He was tempted, He reminded the devil, "it is written." This is an immensely powerful statement. Whenever a person is contesting a case in the court of law, one powerful piece of evidence to boost a person's case is to have things documented (written down). The ink on that paper is timeless and the judge overseeing that case can't help but rule in your favour. The person opposing you has no other choice but to retreat, when they see your evidence "it is written," to your favour. Satan, our adversary, and the tempter needs to be reminded each time in the hour of us being tempted, the evidence is there against you and in my favour because "it is written."

Evicted from The Garden (God's Presence)

The five senses; taste, touch, smell, hearing, and seeing, all report to the carnal mind – which is the enemy of God. These senses are what Satan uses to tempt us! The lust of the flesh includes tasting, touching, smelling, and hearing. The lust of the eyes is seeing. The pride of life is thinking you are special because of who you are, what you have, what you know, or what you look like.

The enemy uses these three things, the lust of the flesh, the lust of the eyes, and the pride of life, to entice us to sin. Scripture shows this process at work in both the Garden of Eden and on the Mount of Temptation.

The carnal mind was the downfall of man in the Garden of Eden. This fall of man resulted in them being evicted from their first home which is a symbol of God's presence. **Genesis 3:8-10, 17, 22-24** [8] *And they heard the voice of the Lord* God walking in the garden in the cool of the day: and Adam and his wife hid themselves from the presence of the Lord God amongst the trees of the garden. ⁹ *And the Lord God called unto Adam, and said unto him, Where art thou?* ¹⁰ *And he said, I heard thy voice in the garden, and I was afraid, because I was naked; and I hid myself...* ²⁴ *So he drove out the man; and he placed at the east of the garden of Eden Cherubims, and a flaming sword which turned every way, to keep the way of the tree of life.*

God placed Adam not just as the husband of his relationship with Eve but as the head of that marriage. As the head of the marriage, Adam had a spiritual responsibility to hold fast to God's commandments. Even if his wife failed to do so, he was expected to be the spiritual leader. Like Job when he was tested and his wife lost faith and began to blaspheme. He had to hold fast to his faith and continue to glorify and pleased God. It was the same with Lot. When his wife became overtaken by the sins and lust of Sodom and Gomorrah and couldn't help but turn her head and became a pillar of salt. As the spiritual leader he had to keep his head straight in the direction of righteousness that God was leading him. Ahab was also called to be a spiritual leader. However, he was too weak and allowed his wife Jezebel to dictate to him.

Leaders, God has called you to lead his people into the path of righteousness. You can't afford to have yourself overtaken with evil. You must have knowledge of God's Word and hold fast to His command. As a leader you must be able to discern between right and wrong. You must be spiritually strong enough to call the right, right and call the wrong, wrong. Unlike Adam you can't be weak to the flesh where you easily give into temptation. You can't be a lover of money and the things of the flesh and believe you are going to be an effective leader. This will result in you being evicted from God's presence.

Sin brings guilt and causes us to want to hide from God's presence. That was the experience of Adam and Eve. Disobeying God's commands had some long-term consequences. These included natural & spiritual death, loss of their Godly image, pain, hard labour and eviction from God's presence.

It was a sad state that they were evicted from the Garden of Eden (God's presence) but it was necessary. God did this in order that mankind didn't spend the rest of their lives in sin without having the opportunity to be redeemed. Had they been allowed to stay in the Garden of Eden in their sinful state and ate of the tree of life, this would have been the consequence. The tree of Life symbolising the Lord Jesus Christ. No sin can enter God's presence. That's another reason they couldn't stay in the Garden. In all of this God still loved mankind.

The Canopy of Your Love

Let the canopy of your love shelter me from,
The lusts, temptations, jealousy and infatuation of this world.
Let the overarching arms of your love,
Protect me from worldly elements that keeps,

The Fall Of Man

Bombarding my mind like a perpetual rain.
Caused me to be seated at your feet,
As I'm firmly anchored in the root of your love.
Planted deep in your grace to the extent,
I'm not swayed by the wind of false and deceitful teaching.
Let me always flourish like a tree planted by the rivers of water.
Each day let me be extended beyond the borders of my enemies,
As I'm fertilised by the ever-flowing sap of your love.
As the golden ray of Your Son shines on me,
Cause me always to bear much fruit,
Like a tree photosynthesizing in all its glory.
Caused my fruit to last, as they stand the test of time,
Like a palm tree, they will nourish generation to generation.
Let there be found healing for the Nations in my fruits,
As the green herb in the Garden of Eden.
Let the canopy of Your love shade me,
From the vehement heat of the problems of this world.
Cause me to find rest in the comfort of your bending branches.
As my roots penetrate the soil that surrounds Your Tree of Life,
Enable me to absorb the nutritious substances,
That will flow through my being.
Resulting in me producing the characteristics which are evident in You.
Let my fruits be that of the Spirit.
Loving as our Heavenly Father, kind as the Good Samaritan, meek as The Lamb,
faithful as a friend, patient as a teacher, peaceful like a dove, joyful as a lark,

Showing goodness as a true disciple, and temperate as an exemplary leader.
All these fruits encapsulated in the canopy of your love.

Copyright © Richard Scott Brown 2022.
Date Written May 8th, 2014. All rights reserved.

CHAPTER 3

The Need For A Spiritual Regeneration

The Spirit of God Leaving King Saul

1 Samuel 15:2-3, 9-11,13-15, 22-24, 26 *² Thus saith the Lord* of hosts, I remember that which Amalek did to Israel, how he laid wait for him in the way, when he came up from Egypt. *³ Now go and smite Amalek, and utterly destroy all that they have, and spare them not; but slay both man and woman, infant and suckling, ox and sheep, camel and ass. ⁹ But Saul and the people spared Agag, and the best of the sheep, and of the oxen, and of the fatlings, and the lambs, and all that was good, and would not utterly destroy them: but everything that was vile and refuse, that they destroyed utterly.* ¹⁰ *Then came the word of the Lord* unto Samuel, saying, ¹¹ *It repents me that I have set up Saul to be king: for he is turned back from following me, and hath not performed* *my commandments. And it grieved Samuel; and he cried unto the Lord all night* . . . ²⁶ *And Samuel said unto Saul, I will not return with thee: for thou hast rejected the word of the Lord, and the Lord* hath rejected thee from being king over Israel.

1 Samuel 16:13-16 ¹³ *Then Samuel took the horn of oil, and anointed him in the midst of his brethren: and the Spirit of the Lord came upon David from that day forward. So, Samuel rose up, and went to Ramah.* ¹⁴ *But the Spirit of the Lord departed from Saul, and an evil spirit from the Lord troubled him.* ¹⁵ *And Saul's servants said unto him, behold now, an evil spirit from God troubles thee* . . .

In verse **2 of 1 Samuel 15** the Prophet Samuel spoke about God remembering what Amalek did to Israel when he came up from Israel. As children of God when we sin and repent of our errors God forgives us. **Micah 7:19**: *"He will again have compassion on us and will subdue our iniquities. You will cast all our sins into the depths of the sea."* However, when an individual who is not in covenant with God does something to a child of God. That person is in trouble with God. God remembers the wrongs wrought against His children. That's why we shouldn't avenge ourselves but rather vengeance is His and He will repay. When we walk in God's truth and obey His commands He will fight on our behalf.

On the other hand, when we choose to walk in disobedience to God's Word, His wrath will turn against us. This was the situation with king Saul. God clearly instructed Saul to get rid of Amalek, utterly destroy all that they have and don't spare anything. Instead he and the children of

The Need For A Spiritual Regeneration

Israel disobeyed God's clear instruction. The lust of the flesh and the lust of the eyes crept in and they chose to save the best of everything and all that was good. This reminds me of the fall of man Genesis 3:6 ⁶ *And when **the woman saw that the tree was good for food**, and that **it was pleasant to the eyes**, and a tree to be desired to make one wise, she took of the fruit thereof, and did eat, and gave also unto her husband with her; and he did eat.* Whenever God says not to do something but our eyes and our flesh gets the better of us and tells us what God forbids us not to do is good for us, we are on the verge of God's judgement. Whenever God says don't touch this or get rid of that, it's because it's not good for us and later it will lead to our destruction.

What was worse in Saul's situation was that the things God told him to get rid of he and the people were bringing to offer up as sacrifice to God. Like the prophet Samuel said to Saul, God takes greater delight in us obeying His Words than offering up sacrifice. There are many people who are walking in disobedience to God's word but when they gather among the congregation, their worship becomes polluted before God. Many people are operating in the spirit of witchcraft because they chose to walk in rebellion to God's Word and His authority that He Has established and don't even know it. Some people are bent on doing things their way and not God's way. This is stubbornness and it is influenced by iniquity and the spirit of idolatry. God is saying it's either His way and His Word if we are going to be led by Him.

The prophet told Saul because he has rejected God's Word, God Has rejected him. I explained in a previous chapter that God is His Word. When we are rejecting God's Word we are in reality rejecting God. There are grave consequences when we choose to operate in this manner. We see Countries that are meant to be Christian countries rejecting God's word and forsaking morality. Be warned God Has rejected you because you have rejected His Word and therefore you Have rejected Him. God's judgement is coming to your doors. Only if you genuinely repent will the judgement stay. One of Saul's lame excuses was that he feared the people and obeyed their voice. What kind of leader are you when you fear the people more than God and choose their word over God's Word? You are not a leader but a follower and don't deserve to be in charge. We need leaders who are guided by the Holy Spirit only and not the voice of a man or a woman.

The grave consequences that Saul experienced was that God rejected him from being king over Israel. That wasn't all but the worst consequence was **1 Samuel 16:14** [14] *But the Spirit of the Lord departed from Saul, and an evil spirit from the Lord troubled him.* When the Spirit of God has departed from a person you become a walking spiritually dead person. The Spirit of God departing from a person is God saying I don't want anything else to do with you. God removing His Spirit from Saul was like Adam and Eve being evicted from the Garden of Eden. The Garden of Eden was where they fellowshipped daily in the presence of the Lord. When they were evicted they were cut off from God's presence and lost their Godly image.

As a child of God, the Spirit of God is what connects us to Him. Without His Spirit we are nothing. **Psalm 16:11** [11] *Thou wilt show me the path of life: in thy presence is fullness of joy; at thy right hand there are pleasures for evermore.* It is in God's presence we will be quickened and empowered. It is in God's presence all of our needs will be supplied according to His riches in Glory. The Scripture tells us that an evil spirit from God troubled Saul after the Spirit of God departed from him. Whenever the Spirit of God leaves us our lives will be taken over by demonic forces. **Luke 11:24-26** [24] *When the unclean spirit is gone out of a man, he walketh through dry places, seeking rest; and finding none, he saith, I will return unto my house whence I came out.* [25] *And when he cometh, he finds it swept and garnished.* [26] *Then he goes, and taketh to him seven other spirits more wicked than himself; and they enter in, and dwell there: and the last state of that man is worse than the first.* This passage explains that the Spirit of God leaving us leaves us in a state that is seven times worse than when we first knew Jesus as our Lord and Saviour. Let us not be fooled. It is either God or the Devil. It's either the Holy Spirit or evil spirits. There is no in between or any middle ground. It took true worship to relieve Saul of the evil spirit that troubled him.

Please Don't Take Your Spirit From Me

David was the chosen vessel the Lord chose to anoint to be king over Israel in Saul's stead. David was a man after God's own heart. This means whatever God's will was, that's what David set his heart to pursue. On the other hand, Saul's heart was fixed on the things that he desired, the things of the flesh. While David pursued the things of the Spirit.

Taken from the backside of the desert where he was the shepherd boy, God used Samuel to anoint him to be king over His people Israel. A cast out from his father's house but God had him in training as a shepherd boy taking care of the sheep, so in the future he could shepherd the children of Israel. When God has ordained and chosen you from before your mother's womb it doesn't matter your family background. When God puts His anointing on you it makes all the difference. God can take you from the pit to the pulpit, from prison to being Prime Minister, from a prostitute to a person who testifies of your encounter with Jesus Christ.

David was able to lead Israel into numerous victories over their many enemies. One of the most notable was against the giant Goliath and the Philistines. While taking care of his flock of sheep, he had great training for future battles by slaying a lion and a bear that came to kill his sheep. Therefore, he was able to fearlessly face Goliath and the Philistine army in the Name of the Lord of Host. David knew God was with him from the manner He allowed him to slay the lion and the bear. When God is with you, and you are abiding in his will, victory is guaranteed.

It was this young David who was also a skilful musician that played skilfully under the anointing and relieved Saul momentarily of being troubled by the evil spirit from the Lord. It shows us that there is a power in anointed praise and worship. Anointed praise and worship are what draws God into our situation. Anointed praise and worship can grant us victory over the enemy like king Jehoshaphat's army. **2 Chronicles 20:20-22** [20] *They got up early in the morning and went out to the desert of Tekoa. When they went out, Jehoshaphat stood and said, "Listen to me, O Judah and the people of Jerusalem. Trust in the Lord your God, and you will be made strong. Trust in the men who speak for Him, and you will do well."* [21] *When he had spoken with the people, he called those who sang to the Lord and those who praised Him in holy clothing. They went out in front of the army and said, "Give thanks to the Lord. For His loving-kindness lasts forever."* [22] *When they began to sing and praise, the Lord set traps against the men of Ammon, Moab, and Mount Seir, who had come against Judah. So, they were destroyed.* There is victory in our praise and worship. Our anointed praise and worship can reverse a negative situation.

    David would have realised the agony Saul endured of having The Spirit of the Lord leaving him and then to be tormented by an evil spirit. Indeed, the very worst thing that can happen to a man is to fall into the hands of the Lord. **Hebrews 10: 30-31**[30] *For we know him that hath said, vengeance belongs unto me, I will recompense, saith the Lord. And again, The Lord shall judge his people.* [31] *It is a fearful thing to fall into the hands of the living God.* When you are able to outrun or hide from a man, unfortunately you can't do the same with God. David summarises it perfectly in **Psalm 139:7-12** [7] *Whither shall I go from thy spirit? or whither shall I flee from thy presence?* [8] *If I ascend up into heaven, thou art there: if I make my bed in hell, behold, thou art there.* [9] *If I take the wings of the morning, and dwell in the uttermost parts of* *the sea;* ¹⁰ *Even there shall thy hand lead me, and thy right hand shall hold me . . .*

There is no place in this Universe we can go and God is not there. He is the Omnipresent one. Therefore, it is best for us to humble ourselves and be obedient to His Word.

David wasn't perfect himself, but he was a man after God's own heart. He didn't always get things right like most of us today, but it was his attitude towards God afterwards. In **2 Samuels 11** David sinned in more than one way against God. He committed adultery with Bathsheba, Uriah's wife. He then murdered Uriah by setting him up to die in the hottest part of the battle. All of these actions of David displeased the Lord. Because of David's actions he brought a curse upon his house according to the prophet Nathan. God told David because what he did was in secret, but his punishment will be before all Israel. **2 Samuel 12:13-14** ¹³ *And David said unto Nathan, I have sinned against the Lord. And Nathan said unto David, The Lord also has put away thy sin; thou shalt not die.* ¹⁴ *Howbeit, because by this deed thou hast given great occasion to the enemies of the Lord to blaspheme, the child also that is born unto thee shall surely die.*

When confronted by the prophet Nathan, David genuinely showed remorse and God saw his heart. That's why the prophet said "the Lord also has put away thy sin; thou shall not die. Unlike Saul when confronted by the Prophet Samuel, he didn't show genuine remorse. He lied to say he did what God commanded him to do. Instead of genuinely repenting, Saul was instead asking the prophet to honour him in front of the elders and all Israel. These actions reflect the characteristics of someone who was very proud and a proud heart comes before a fall.

Even though David genuinely repented there were long term consequences for his actions. When we put God's Name into disrepute and cause people to blaspheme, God doesn't take kindly to this. David's child with Bathsheba ended up dying and there was discord in David's house.

In **Psalm 51** we see where it is outlined how David went about his repentance after his sinful act with Bathsheba. **Psalm 51:1-11,16-17** *Have mercy upon me, O God, according to thy lovingkindness: according unto the multitude of thy tender mercies blot out my transgressions.* [2] *Wash me thoroughly from mine iniquity, and cleanse me from my sin.* [3] *For I acknowledge my transgressions: and my sin is ever before me.* [4] *Against thee, thee only, have I sinned, and done this evil in thy sight: that thou might be justified when thou speak and be clear when thou judge.* [5] *Behold, I was shaped in iniquity; and in sin did my mother conceive me . . .* [10] *Create in me a clean heart, O God; and renew a right spirit within me.* [11] *Cast me not away from thy presence; and take not thy holy spirit from me . . .*

David showed genuine remorse, unlike Saul. He acknowledged his transgressions. True repentance is to be able to humbly own up to the wrongs we did. The scripture tells us about the publican and the Pharisees who went up to the temple to pray. The Pharisees exalted himself while the publican humbled himself and acknowledged his wrongs. It was his prayers that God answered.

David asked God to wash him thoroughly from his iniquity and cleanse him from his sins. Sin is the actual transgression (breaking) of the law. In simple terms sin is displeasing God. Iniquity is the evil, born in us, that breeds transgression. Iniquities are the sinful habits and traits we have inherited from our forefathers which have been passed down to us. Adam sinned and passed on his iniquity to all mankind **(Genesis 5:3** . . . *[3] And Adam lived one hundred and thirty years, and begot a son in his own likeness, after his image, and named him Seth)*. This inbred iniquity is also called "the Old Man." And "the body of sin." It is clear in this passage that David said that his mother conceived him in sin. Was it that he was born out of wedlock (as some theologians might suggest) for him to acknowledge that he was conceived in sin? Or the fact that we have all sinned and come short of God's glory since the fall of man? As the younger of Jesse's son's David found himself in the bushes taking care of the sheep while his older brothers were elsewhere occupied. In **Psalm 27** David said, "when my mother and father forsake me then the Lord will take me up." It shows David felt some form of rejection being the youngest child, yet he was the one who had to take care of the sheep. However, God has a sense of humour, what may have felt like a state of rejection for David, in God's eyes he was in training to lead a great nation.

In **Psalm 51: 10** David asked God to create in him a clean heart and renew a right spirit within him. He realised that the condition of his heart influenced his evil actions. It should be our prayer each day for God to create in us clean hearts and renew a right spirit within us. David's son Solomon caught the vision years later and wrote in **Proverbs 4:23** [23] *Keep (guard) thy heart with all diligence; for out of it are the issues of life.* We have a responsibility to keep watch over our heart because the issues of our lives flow from it. Be it good or evil actions, they were born in our heart. That is the reason the Psalmist wrote in **Psalm 119:11** [11] *Thy word have I hid in mine heart, that I might not sin against thee.* This is such a powerful passage. Our heart controls the flow of the issues of our lives but hiding God's Word in our hearts will enable us not to sin against God. When we have the Word of God planted in our inner man it will be difficult for us to sin against God. David was overtaken by lust and forsook God's Word.

Not only are our actions influenced by what goes in and out of our heart but also the Holy Spirit and unclean spirits. If we feed our spirit man with the Word of God we will be directed by the Holy Spirit. However, if we feed our flesh, we leave the door open for unclean spirits to come in and influence our actions. The Scripture tells us to walk in the Spirit and we will not fulfil the lust of the flesh. David realised it wasn't the Holy Spirit that caused him to commit all those evil acts. He instead recognises he was being influenced by the wrong spirit. That's the reason he asked God to renew a right spirit in him.

David was around and observed what happened to Saul when he sinned against God and the Lord withdrew His Spirit from him. He became troubled by an evil spirit from the Lord. He observed Saul in action and realised he was a walking spiritual dead man. David now finds himself in a state of sinning against God. Not wanting to experience what Saul had experienced he cried out to God in **Psalm 51:11** *Cast me not away from thy presence; and take not thy Holy Spirit from me.* He knew it was in God's presence there's fullness of joy. He knew he could only thrive in God's Holy presence. Most importantly David saw what Saul had to endure and was determined for God not to take His Holy Spirit from him. He did not want to experience being a walking spiritual dead man. David knew that it was in the Lord that he lived, moved and had his existence. He knew that without the Spirit of God the victories he experienced in battles he would not achieve them. This was truly a man after God's own heart, he realised without being in God's will, his life would be in vain. Adam and Eve got evicted from God's presence, their Godly image was lost. God's presence and His Holy Spirit are both key for us to live a successful life that will bring glory and honour to God's great Name.

You Must Be Born again

John 3:1-4 *There was a man of the Pharisees, named Nicodemus, a ruler of the Jews:* ² *The same came to Jesus by night, and said unto him, Rabbi, we know that thou art a teacher come from God: for no man can do these miracles that thou does except God be with him.* ³ *Jesus answered and said unto him, Verily, verily, I say unto thee, except a man be born again, he cannot see the kingdom of God.* ⁴ *Nicodemus saith unto him, how can a man be born when he is old? can he enter the second time into his mother's womb, and be* *born?* Nicodemus was a prominent Jew. He was a ruler. This shows he had a level of authority. Him coming to Jesus by night shows that he had been observing Him in ministry. Nicodemus made a very profound statement. He said we know that thou art a teacher come from God. He didn't say Jesus was sent from God. Jesus coming (begotten) from God shows that He was God in the flesh and the miracles He did proves this. Even as Nicodemus confirmed. Everything Nicodemus said to Jesus was correct and you may think that Jesus would have responded by telling him thank you for your compliment. However, Jesus realised that Nicodemus' focus was on the miracles, which is not a bad thing. Jesus knew there was something much more important than seeing the miracles performed and that's why He quickly changed the conversion about being born again in order to see God's Kingdom. As it relates to being born again, it should be noted as in the natural so in the spiritual. When a baby is being born firstly the woman's water breaks, the umbilical cord supplies life giving blood, oxygen (wind, air, spirit, life) and other important nutrients to the baby until the baby takes its first breath.

How many people have observed many miracles, signs and wonders but you are not born again? How many people are in church every Sunday or Saturday and other days of the week, but you are not born again? Some people are only there because they have a relationship with the leader, and they think that's enough to get them to Heaven. A person can receive prophecies, see the prophecies fulfilled in their lives, experienced miracles upon miracles but still miss the mark because "They haven't been born again." Remember

God causes the rain to fall upon the just and the unjust. The children of Israel experienced God's miraculous hands in their Exodus from Egypt and on their journey to the Promised Land. Yet some of them never entered the Promised Land because of disobedience. The miracles are for others but being born again is personal. It's a personal decision. When you see the signs, wonders and miracles happening around you, it's God doing what He has promised but have you made the personal decision to accept the Lord Jesus Christ as your Saviour by becoming born again?

As Jesus explained to Nicodemus, being born again is not a grown individual entering into their mother's womb a second time but instead having a spiritual rebirth or being born from above. The fall of man left a spiritual void as Adam and Eve lost their Godly image. When one is born again this spiritual void gets filled and the Godly image that was lost becomes restored. Jesus emphasised the point and the importance of it: you must be born again when he said to Nicodemus "marvel (be amazed) not that I said unto thee, you must be born again." Above everything in this life God wants us to know that being born again should be the number one priority. If we are going to partake and function in God's Kingdom "we must be born again." Until we become born again, we'll still be operating outside of God's presence and functioning without His Spirit. In essence until we become born again, we are walking spiritually dead people. The Lord Jesus wanted Nicodemus to know that this was the New Covenant. Even though the Jews were traditionally God's chosen people, in this New Covenant they must be born again. Whether you are rich, poor, young, middle aged, old or whatever nationality, you must be born again in this New Covenant.

When Adam and Eve fell, God had in mind for their generations to be redeemed through the Lamb of God who was slain before the foundations of the world. In the process of redemption, we must be born again. That's the reason they were evicted from the Garden of Eden in order that they didn't partake of the Tree of Life in their sinful state. If they did, the opportunity to be redeemed and born again would have been lost. God is the Omniscience God who knows the end from the beginning. He knew before he created man they would fall. It came as no surprise to him. That's the reason the Lamb of God was slain before the foundations of the world. In all of this it proves God's eternal love for mankind. For God so loved the world, that He gave His only begotten Son. That whosoever believes in Him will not perish but have everlasting life. God does not take pleasure in the death of a sinner or unbeliever.

Born of The Water

Water is essential for life to exist on Earth. It exists as a solid, liquid, and gas and is common in every state. Covering about seventy-five percent of the Earth's surface and up to ninety percent of mass in living organisms, water is the most abundant liquid on Earth.

Water is mentioned a total of seven hundred and twenty-two times in the Bible, more often than faith, hope, prayer, and worship. In the Bible, it doesn't take long for water to be mentioned. Right away in **Genesis 1:2**, "The earth was a formless void and darkness covered the face of the deep, the Spirit of God swept over the face of the waters." Water is such an essential component of life, it was created on the very first day.

In both the Old and New Testaments, the word "water" is used for salvation and eternal life, which God offers humankind through faith in his **Son**. In **John 4:10-15**, part of Jesus' dialogue with the Samaritan woman at the well, he speaks symbolically of His salvation as "living water" and as "a spring of water welling up to eternal life."

Following this same theme, water sometimes symbolises the spiritual cleansing that comes with the acceptance of God's offer of salvation **(Ezek 36:25)**. In fact, in Ephesians 5:26, the "water" that does the cleansing of the bride, the church, is directly tied in with God's Word, of which it is a symbol.

In order to understand why water was chosen for washing and renewal in the Sacrament of Baptism, we should remember that ever since the beginning, in the story of creation, there has been an association between water and life.

The Holy Bible says: "And the Spirit of God was hovering over the face of the waters" **(Gen.1: 2)**. And God said: "Let the waters abound with an abundance of living creatures, and let birds fly above the earth across the face of the firmament of the heavens" **(Gen.1: 20)**. Thus, life sprang out of water and we can see the connection between water, life and the Spirit of God.

We also read in the Old Testament that God likens Himself to water when He reproached the people saying: "They have forsaken Me, the fountain of living waters, and hewn themselves cisterns - broken cisterns that can hold no water" (**Jer.2: 13**). This association is also mentioned in the words of the Lord Jesus Christ: " 'He who believes in Me, as the Scripture has said, out of his heart will flow rivers of living water.' By this He spoke concerning the Spirit, whom those believing in Him would receive" (**John.7: 38,39**).

Therefore, water is a symbol of life and sometimes of the Holy Spirit Himself. The words in **Psalm 1:1-3** are Divinely inspired "He shall be like a tree planted by the rivers of water, that brings forth its fruit in its season." The fruit is the fruit of the Holy Spirit.

The connections between water, life and the Holy Spirit in the Holy Bible commence from Genesis (**Gen.1: 2**) and continue until the end of the Book of Revelation: "I will give the fountain of the water of life freely to him who thirsts" (**Rev.21:6**), "And he showed me a pure river of water of life, clear as crystal, proceeding from the throne of God and of the Lamb" (**Rev.22: 1**) and "...let him who thirsts come. And whoever desires, let him take the water of life freely" (**Rev.22: 17**). Water flows throughout the scripture, and this should remind us of its importance . . . both spiritually and physically. In the crossing of the Red Sea, the water symbolises life and death together; death of the servile man and life of the free man who came up out of the water.

John 3:5 [5] *Jesus answered, Verily, verily, I say unto thee, except a man be born of water and of the Spirit, he cannot* *enter into the kingdom of God.* Being born of water is referring to water baptism as God ordained. Baptism is an important event in the believer's walk with Jesus Christ. This is a sensitive subject in Christendom.

Water Baptism is a holy act commanded by God's Word. In baptism, the body of the believer is submerged (dipped, immersed, plunged) completely under water. In this act of obedience and faith, the believer is identifying himself with the death, burial, and resurrection of the Lord Jesus Christ (**Romans 6:3-6**). After repenting of sins and putting faith in Jesus Christ, getting water baptised is what God expects a person to do? I'm going to make what would appear to be a controversial point yet when it has sunk in it will be very profound. A person's salvation is tied up in identifying with the death, burial and resurrection of the Lord Jesus Christ which comes through water baptism. It's not His birth we identify with in water baptism. That's why the Apostles didn't emphasise Christ's Birth. The purpose of Him being born was to die, bury and resurrect after three days to bring salvation to the whole world. All the other so-called gods were born and died but only the Lord Jesus Christ resurrected from the dead. The Apostles therefore preached about a resurrected Jesus Christ.

Nowadays there is more emphasis placed on Christ's Birth (so-called Christmas, Christ wasn't born on December 25th) rather than the importance of water baptism. Be it known, a person can celebrate Christ's Birth all 365 or 366 days of the year but if you don't identify with His death, burial, and resurrection through water baptism you are not assured salvation. I can hear somebody say, "but what about the thief on the Cross?" The answer to that question is this. The Thief on the Cross along with Jesus's Crucifixion was a different dispensation compared to the dispensation of the Church of Jesus Christ (the Church started on the Day of Pentecost). Even though they were only fifty days apart. The tearing of the veil (which was after the death of Jesus Christ/He gave up the ghost) ended one dispensation. On the Day of Pentecost, the dispensation of the Church of the Lord Jesus Christ and the Last Days commenced.

Genuine repentance and water baptism in the Name of the Lord Jesus or Jesus Christ (throughout the Book of Acts, there was no mention of the titles "Father, Son and Holy Spirit in water baptism) were the requirements to become a member of the Church of the Lord Jesus Christ, in this new dispensation (this dispensation continues until the Church of the Lord Jesus Christ is taken out of the world). That's the reason the Lord Jesus Himself showed us the example of being water baptised, even though he didn't sin, and neither was He in need of salvation.

Anyone who will repent (turn to Christ) and believe the Gospel of Jesus Christ can be baptised. It is not scriptural to baptise babies as some very large so-called church organisations do because they are not mature enough to repent and believe in the Lord Jesus Christ. A baby cannot take the step of repentance, nor can he/she understand enough to believe in the Lord. There is no Bible command to baptise babies. There are many Bible examples of the requirements of who can be baptised. What Jesus taught His disciples to do was to take the babies in their hands and bless them (what we call dedicate).

When a person becomes baptised in water. Numerous things are accomplished in that individual. 1) **We receive the Remission of Sins**

Acts 2:38 Then Peter said unto them, Repent, and be baptised every one of you in the name of Jesus Christ for the remission of sins, and ye shall receive the gift of the Holy Ghost, 2) **We bury the "Old Man"- the nature of sin. Rom 6:6** knowing this, that our old man was crucified with Him, that the body of sin might be done away with, that we should no longer be slaves of sin. In a true experience of water baptism: 3) **We experience a New Birth of Resurrection Life.**

John 3:5 Jesus answered, "Most assuredly, I say to you, unless one is born of water and the Spirit, he cannot enter the kingdom of God.

Romans 6:5,11 [5] *For if we have been planted together in the likeness of his death, we shall be also in the likeness of his resurrection.* [11] *Likewise reckon ye also yourselves to be dead indeed unto sin, but alive unto God through Jesus Christ our Lord.* 4) **We receive the Circumcision of Heart.** **Colossians 2:11-12.** [11] *In whom also ye are circumcised with the circumcision made without hands, in putting off the body of the sins of the flesh by the circumcision of Christ:* [12] *Buried with him in baptism, wherein also ye are risen with him through the faith of the operation of God, who hath raised him from the dead.*

The Need For A Spiritual Regeneration

5) We are placed into the Body of Christ- the Church. **1 Corinthians 12:13** *For by one Spirit we were all baptized into one body—whether Jews or Greeks, whether slaves or free—and have all been made to drink [g]into one Spirit.*

Romans 6:3 *Or do you not know that as many of us were baptised into Christ Jesus were baptised into His death?*

The Remission of Sins is the separating of the sin from the sinner. We may ask forgiveness of our individual sins which we have committed; but the sinful nature we have inherited from Adam and our fore-parents must be destroyed by death. 1) There can be no remission of sin without the shedding of blood (death), for death is the penalty (payment, punishment) for sin. **Hebrews 9:22.** 2) The death of Jesus Christ made possible the remission of sins for us. He paid the penalty for our sins.

Matthew 26:28 For this is My blood of the new covenant, which is shed for many for the remission of sins. **3)** When repentant believers are baptised into Christ, they receive the remission of sins.

Luke 24:47 *and that repentance and remission of sins should be preached in His name to all nations, beginning at Jerusalem.*

Acts 2:38 *Then Peter said to them, "Repent, and let every one of you be baptised in the name of Jesus Christ for the remission of sins; and you shall receive the gift of the Holy Spirit.* There were instances in Scripture where people received the baptism of the Holy Spirit first. However, they received water baptism in the Name of the Lord Jesus afterwards (**Acts 10:44-48**). This shows the importance of water baptism because it is a command while the baptism of the Holy Spirit is a promise from God. Another important point to deduce from this is that the baptism of the Holy Spirit signifies that a person is anointed and gifted. Therefore, it doesn't matter how anointed and gifted you are, you must identify yourself with Christ through the baptism of water in the Name of the Lord Jesus.

A lot of people believe water baptism is a New Testament thing. However just like the Old Testament was a shadow of things to come in the New Testament, there were events of water baptism in the Old Testament, that were a foreshadow of water baptism in the New Testament. The apostle Peter talks about Noah's flood, and specifically tells us that New Testament baptism "corresponds to this. **1 Peter 3: 20-22** [19] *By which also he went and preached unto the spirits in prison;*[20] *Which sometime were disobedient, when once the longsuffering of God waited in the days of Noah, while the ark was a preparing, wherein few, that is, eight souls were saved by water.* [21] *The like figure (Figuratively this is like baptism) whereunto even baptism does also now save (which also save us now) us (not the putting away of the filth of the flesh, but the answer of a good conscience toward God,) by the resurrection of Jesus Christ:*

[22] *Who is gone into heaven and is on the right hand of God; angels and authorities and powers being made subject unto him.*

Some people are adamant that baptism doesn't save us but here the Apostle Peter who was God's mouthpiece on the Day of Pentecost, clearly states that baptism does save us now. Water baptism doesn't wash away the dirt and filth of our skin. Instead, it is our sin nature that we inherit from Adam that is being washed away. Some people will be upset with me now because I've messed up their theo-lie-ogy (theology). **Proverbs 30:5-6** *⁵ Every word of God is pure: he is a shield unto them that put their trust in him. ⁶ Add thou not unto his words, lest he reprove thee, and thou be found a liar.* **Revelation 22:18-19** *¹⁸ For I testify unto every man that heareth the words of the prophecy of this book, If any man shall add unto these things, God shall add unto him the plagues that are written in this book: ¹⁹ And if any man shall take away from the words of the book of this prophecy, God shall take away his part out of the book of life, and out of the holy city, and from the things which are written in this book.*

When it comes to reading and understanding God's Word, we shouldn't come with our own thoughts and information from theological seminary or doctrine of church organisations. The natural man cannot understand the things of God because they are spiritually discerned. Unfortunately, many people approach the Word of God with their fleshly mind and in the process creates confusion by wrongly dividing the word of truth. They in turn add and take away from God's word. By doing this they are endangering their soul to Hell. I will elaborate more on God's Word in chapter 6. The fact is many church organisations are established on false doctrines which is not God's will for us. He shall know the truth and the truth shall set you free.

The children of Israel crossing the Red Sea to enter the Promised Land was also a type of water baptism that was to come in the New Testament. **1 Corinthians 10:1-9** *Moreover, brethren, I would not that ye should be ignorant, how that all our fathers were under the cloud, and all passed through the sea;* [2] *And were all baptised unto Moses in the cloud and in the sea;* [3] *And did all eat the same spiritual meat;* [4] *And did all drink the same spiritual drink: for they drank of that spiritual Rock that followed them: and that Rock was Christ.* [5] *But with many of them God was not well pleased: for they were overthrown in the wilderness.*

Analysing this passage, we see that the children of Israel crossing the Red Sea was a type of water baptism. In the New Testament water baptism is the second process of salvation. The first requirement is that we repent and believe in the Lord Jesus, and this is a command, "repent and be baptised everyone of you in the Name of Jesus Christ for the remission of your sins..." However, we see getting water baptised is not the end of the process of being saved. We are required to live a life of holiness as born-again believers. Without holiness no man shall see God. After the children of Israel crossed the Red Sea and journeyed into the wilderness, thousands of them lusted after evil things. With this God was not well pleased. He overthrew (killed) them (twenty-three thousand) in the wilderness. All of this has been written as an example and a guide to the New Testament church. Can you imagine after having a spiritual encounter with Christ (Who was the Rock they drank from) in the wilderness and seeing the miraculous hands of God, some of them still went lusting after the flesh. This is a typical example of the human nature. The writer of Romans says, when I want to do good evil is present with me. This lets me know, no matter how we have encountered God's power and see His wondrous works, we are surrounded by evil and temptations. It is only by His grace we are standing today, it's no good thing that you and I have done. There is no one that is good, except God. However, we must make the personal choice that we are going to choose righteousness over a lifestyle of sinful pleasures.

God expects us as His children each day to overcome the lust of the flesh and walk in the Spirit. The ones who will be truly saved are those that will endure to the end. It's not just how we start that will bring us salvation. God expects us to complete the process. I've seen people being Holy Ghost filled and water baptised, some of them were even baptised with the Holy Ghost first before water baptism. However, they have left the faith and started lusting after evil things. The doctrine of once saved you are always saved is also a ginormous lie from the pit of Hell. God wants His children to be taught how to be able to endure hardship as a good soldier of Christ, but Satan wants us to believe any and everything goes with God and He will turn a blind eye to it.

There is a reason the word of God instructs us to abstain from sexual immorality (fornication, adultery, homosexuality etc). These immoral acts are like a type of self-worship (self-glorification) that God hates and come in a similar category as idolatry. In fact, when a born-again believer becomes entangled with these lifestyles, their ministry will be hindered, and it blocks the flow of the Holy Spirit. That's why Paul teaches us that we should flee fornication, youthful lust, and idolatry. Just like Joseph in Potiphar's house, sometimes when the enemy wants to trap us, we may have to run leave some of our possessions behind and shun the very appearance of evil. This is where self-control which is a part of the fruit of the Spirit comes into play. It doesn't matter how anointed a person is. God cares more about the fruit of the Spirit in that person's life rather than the gift. The gift of the Spirit is to edify others, but the fruit is what shows our relationship with God. Let us therefore don't judge a person's Christian walk by how gifted or anointed they are but rather how much the fruit of the Spirit is evident in their lives. Remember even Lucifer was anointed, and Satan is still gifted and can work miracles. It would be a crying shame for someone to preach others into the Kingdom of God, while they become a castaway. Resulting in their soul being lost. The more gifted and anointed a person is, it's the more they need to consecrate and humble themselves (through prayer and fasting) and aspire to living a life of holiness, without which no man shall see God.

In the structure and layout of the Tabernacle in the Old Testament, there were three sections. These were the Outer Court, the Inner Court (Holy place and the Holy of Holies. Situated on the Outer Court were the Brazen Altar and the Laver basin. The Altar was to offer sacrifice by the priest, and this was symbolic of the sacrificial work that Christ as the Lamb of God who slain before the foundation of the world had to do on Calvary's Cross.

The Need For A Spiritual Regeneration   87

For the Priest to enter the Holy Place and the Holy of holies, he first had to wash himself in the laver basin. This symbolises water baptism, one of the requirements to gain access into the Church of Jesus Christ. It is in water baptism that a person identifies with the sacrificial work of Christ on the Cross and His death, burial, and resurrection. Just as the priest had to first wash himself to enter the Holy Place and perform his priestly duty, that's how we are required to first be washed through water baptism in the Name of Jesus Christ to carry out our duty as a "royal priesthood" in the Church of the Lord Jesus Christ. That means no one (be it best friend or family) should be allowed to serve in the local church in any capacity until one has undergone water baptism. In the words of the Lord Jesus Christ, "you must be born again."

At the inception of the early church there was such an emphasis, an importance and an urgency placed on water baptism. Immediately as people were convicted and believed as they heard the gospel preached, they received water baptism. "See here is water can does hinder me to be baptised." Nowadays some church organisations are having so-called baptismal classes for weeks and months before a candidate is baptised. This is unscriptural and nowhere to be found in Scripture. The Apostles understood the importance of water baptism, hence the emphasis and urgency. That emphasis and urgency has been replaced by "being saved by repeating a so-called sinner's prayer and so-called baptismal classes." The Apostles practises were, upon a person's conviction, confession and belief, they were immediately baptised in the Name of the Lord Jesus or the Name of Jesus Christ in water, persons weren't left alone to carry on by themselves, instead they had daily fellowship with the brethren, continuing in the Apostles doctrine, prayers and breaking of bread. This is how they were discipled. That's why there was such numerical and spiritual growth in the early church. When compared to the practises of many church organisations today, there is much to be desired.

Born of the Spirit

John 3:5-7 [5] *Jesus answered, Verily, verily, I say unto thee, except a man be born of water and of the Spirit, he cannot enter into the kingdom of God.* [6] *That which is born of the flesh is flesh; and that which is born of the Spirit is spirit.* [7] *Marvel not that I said unto you, you must be born again.* [8] *The wind blows where it wishes, and you hear the sound thereof, but cannot tell where it comes, and where it goes: so is every one that is born of the Spirit.*

To be born of the Spirit is a part of the process of being born again whereby a person is being baptised (infilled) with the Holy Spirit. The Holy Spirit is God and is also referred to as the Breath (Wind) of God. In nature when a baby is born and the umbilical cord is being cut, it is then expected for that baby to take its first breath. It is in taking that first breath that will enable that baby to take other breaths and continue to do so until the day they die. While in the mother's womb, the baby was supplied with air through the umbilical cord. Without that air (wind) the baby would have died. Whenever a person experiences some form of accident

The Need For A Spiritual Regeneration

and aid is requested for that person, the first question that is asked is "are they breathing?" To be able to breathe is a sign of life.

When God formed man (body) from the dust of the earth, he laid there lifeless until God breathed into his nostrils the breath (spirit) of life and he became a living soul (being, human being). Man did not come alive until God breathed Himself (His Spirit) into him. That's why Luke wrote in **Acts 17:28-31** [28] *for in Him we live and move and have our being, as also some of your own poets have said, 'For we are also His offspring.'* [29] *Therefore, since we are the offspring of God, we ought not to think that the Divine Nature is like gold or silver or stone, something shaped by art and man's devising...* As the first man Adam had his being (soul, became alive) not until God breathed into him, so it is with us that until we experience being born of the Spirit, we are spiritually dead or disconnected from our Creator. Adam was God's offspring because God breathed Himself (Spirit) in him. We are Adam's offspring which then makes us God's offspring, only that we inherited Adam's image and are therefore spiritually dead. This condition that we find ourselves in created the need to be "born of the Spirit."

Whenever a person is born of the Spirit, they become connected to God. In other words, from a state of being spiritually dead to a state of being quickened (made alive) by the Spirit. A day of Judgement has been appointed and the assurance for this is that God has raised The Lord Jesus Christ from the dead. Jesus died not necessarily because they killed Him but the fact that "He gave up the Ghost (Spirit)."

When this happened, we had a separation of Divinity (Holy Spirit- God) from Humanity (body and soul). His body was laid in the grave for three days, the Spirit of God that was in Him went into Hell, took the keys of death and Hell, preached to the spirits of the saints.

After the three days and nights were spent in the grave fulfilling prophecies, the Holy Spirit went back into the body, causing Him to be resurrected from the grave in the resurrection power of the Holy Ghost with a glorified body. This proves then for us to become spiritually resurrected we need the Holy Spirit to come upon and inside us. Many of us are walking around but we are spiritually dead. God wants to resurrect us so we can once again be spiritually connected to Him and therefore be able to worship Him. God is a Spirit and they that worship Him must worship Him in spirit and in truth. The Holy Spirit wants to connect to our spirit.

When Jesus went into Hell and took the keys of death and Hell, He created the opportunity for mankind to be relieved of the death sentence that was pronounced on them in the Garden of Eden. "For the day you eat of it, you shall surely die." This death sentence was both in the natural and in the spiritual. On the Cross as he gave up the Ghost the veil in the Temple was ripped in two. This signifying that spiritual access was once again granted to the common man, whatever race, or country they are from. The spiritual access to The Father can only be found in Jesus Christ who is the Way, Truth and Life.

When we place our faith in the risen Christ, a divine transaction takes place **(2 Corinthians 5:21).** God removes

The Need For A Spiritual Regeneration

from us the sin, guilt, and condemnation we deserved because of our rebellion against Him. He throws our sin as far as the east is from the west **(Psalm 103:12)**. At the moment of repentance and faith, the Holy Spirit breathes new life into us, and our bodies become His temple (1 Corinthians 3:16). Our spirits can now commune with God's Spirit as He assures us that we belong to Him **(Romans 8:16)**.

We might think of the human spirit like a deflated balloon that hangs lifeless inside our hearts. We are scarcely aware of its existence until God calls our names and an awakening begins. When we respond to God's call with repentance and faith in what Jesus Christ has done for salvation, we are born of the Spirit. At that point the balloon inflates. The Holy Spirit moves into our spirits and fills us. He begins His transforming work so that we begin to resemble Jesus (2 Corinthians 5:17; Romans 8:29).

There are only two types of people in the world: those who are born of the Spirit and those who are not. In the end, only those two categories matter **(John 3:3)**. That which is born of the flesh is flesh and that which is born of the Spirit is spirit. When we are born of the flesh we will pursue the lust of the flesh, the lust of the eyes and the pride of life. In so doing we will produce all the works of the flesh. When we lead a life of pursuing the desires of the flesh, we cannot understand the things of God because they are spiritually discerned. When we are born of the Spirit, and we choose to walk in the Spirit our flesh becomes subjected to the things of the Spirit. Being born of the Spirit and walking in the Spirit makes us unpredictable like the wind, the devil can't tell where we are going or coming from. Our earthly lives are extended opportunities for us to respond to God's call and become born of the Spirit **(Hebrews 3:15).**

The Untangling Of My Chains

It was like a fountain burst on my inside.
I had to swallow my shame and pride.
Going down memory lane,
It wasn't an easy ride.
I had a good look at myself,
I glanced deep and wide.

In sin my mother conceived me,
I was shaped in iniquity.
Inheriting my fore-parents nature,
Eternal damnation was my destiny.
Fulfilling the lust of the flesh,
Sinning was my hobby.
My end was sure doom,
But before the world's foundation,
Jesus died on Calvary.

At a younger age,
In my ways I was set.
Because of past rejection,
Certain characters I wouldn't accept.
Determined not to be bitten twice,
So-called friends I wouldn't let.
Discriminating against me,
Defending myself,
Against me you wouldn't bet.

The Need For A Spiritual Regeneration

I struggled with pain and bitterness,
I would erupt like a volcano.
Tell me to simmer down,
I was hotter than an inferno.
If I believed I was right,
Like a dog with its bone,
I wouldn't let go.
There were times I was by myself,
I was considered too slow.

The Holy Spirit knocked on my heart,
I opened the door.
He rebuked my every lofty thought,
I was brought to the floor.
Testifying of God's grace and mercy,
My eye water pour.
Ninety-nine and a half was not enough,
Of me He required more.

I realise a calling on my life,
But my past was an hinderance.
Determined to be at full flow,
I sought healing and deliverance.
This experience was refreshing,
It's like I had a second chance.
It was the untangling of my chains,
Again, I'm free to dance.

Being cut off from my evil roots,
I now have the helmet of salvation.
My mind is renewed,
I'm a new creation.

I'm anointed for service,
To bring God's peace to the nations.
With an urgency to transform lives,
No more procrastination.

My shackles are removed,
I have found rest.
Through life's disruption,
I've withstood the test.
Unburnt by the fire,
I've come out God's best.
Free from my past,
I'm free from unrest.

Thy Kingdom come,
Forever God reigns.
In my heart He's now glorified,
I'm now healed from past pain.
Written in the volume of the books,
I have a new name.
I'm free to accomplish my purpose,
Because of,
The untangling of my chains.

Date written: September 28, 2008.
Inspiration: Going to Ellel Ministries (Glynley Manor) for healing and deliverance

Copyright © 2022. Richard Scott Brown. All rights reserved.

CHAPTER 4
The Valley Of Dry Bones Experience

Ezekiel 37 :1-14 *The hand of the Lord came upon me and brought me out in the Spirit of the Lord and set me down in the midst of the valley; and it was full of bones.* ² *Then He caused me to pass by them all around, and behold, there were very many in the open valley; and indeed, they were very dry.* ³ *And He said to me, "Son of man, can these bones live?" So I answered, "O Lord God, You know."* ⁴ *Again He said to me, "Prophesy to these bones, and say to them, 'O dry bones hear the word of the Lord!* ⁵ *Thus says the Lord God to these bones: "Surely I will cause breath (**life**) to enter into you, and you shall live . . .* ¹⁴ *I will put My Spirit in you, and you shall live, and I will place you in your own land. Then you shall know that I, the Lord, have spoken it and performed it," says the Lord.'*

Valley of Dry Bones (spiritual cemetery)

This vision in **Ezekiel 37: 1-14** is one of the most remarkable in the book of Ezekiel. In the previous chapter God had promised the restoration of the nation of Israel and now by this vision sets it forth more concretely. **Ezekiel 36:23-29** [23] *And I will sanctify My great name, which has been profaned among the nations, which you have profaned in their midst; and the nations shall know that I am the Lord," says the Lord God, "when I am hallowed in you before their eyes.* [24] *For I will take you from among the nations, gather you out of all countries, and bring you into your own land.* [25] *Then I will sprinkle clean water on you, and you shall be clean; I will cleanse you from all your filthiness and from all your idols.* [26] *I will give you a new heart and put a new spirit within you; I will take the heart of stone out of your flesh and give you a heart of flesh.* [27] *I will put My Spirit within you and cause you to walk in My statutes, and you will keep My judgements and do them . . .*

Israel was brought into captivity because of their disobedience to the Word of God and their idolatrous behaviour. This sinful behaviour resulted in God's great Name being profaned in their midst. All the chastisement they received was not necessarily about them but rather about God's Holy Name that they profaned wherever they went. God promised them that He would sanctify His Great Name among the nations. We need to realise that even though God has exalted His Word above His Name, it doesn't mean we should take His Name lightly. Scripture reminds us that we should not take the Name of the Lord in vain. This lets me know it's not just calling God's Name in vain that can profane His Great Name but rather when we as people who professed to be children of God act in a manner that will cause unbelievers to blaspheme God's Name. That's the situation David found himself in when he committed adultery with Bathsheba. He caused the heathen nations around to blaspheme the Name of the Lord because of this act God struck the baby dead. God wants us as His people to get to a place where we truly recognise that as our Father who art in Heaven Hallowed be thy Name.

God made the promise to Israel that He would bring them back in their land when He is being hallowed (revered, consecrated) in them amongst the nations. The promise didn't end there but God goes on to say that He would sprinkle clean water upon them so that they may be clean and cleanse them from all their filthiness and idolatry. This symbolises water baptism and the remission of sins. God said that he would give them a new heart and put a right spirit within them. This was the prayer David prayed in **Psalm 51** as he repented of his ungodly actions in committing adultery and murder. As the children of God our heart must be right before Him, and we must have the right spirit within us. **Psalm 24:3-5** [3] *Who may ascend into the hill of the Lord? Or who may stand in His holy place?* [4] *He who has clean hands and a pure heart, who has not lifted up his soul to an idol, Nor sworn deceitfully.* [5] *He shall receive blessing from the Lord, And righteousness from the God of his salvation.* David is letting us know as a man who was after God's own heart that in order for us to be able to enter into God's presence and receive His blessings, we must have clean hands and a pure heart. God also promised to put His Spirit within the children of Israel in order that they may keep his judgements and walk in His statues. When all these conditions are met then they will dwell in the land and be His people while He will be their God. The putting of the Spirit within the children of Israel symbolises the baptism of the Holy Spirit.

Disobedience to God's Word was the reason Israel was taken out of their homeland (the Promised Land) and put in captivity in Babylon. This bears some similarity with Adam and Eve being evicted from the Garden of Eden (God's Presence, their home). In captivity the children of Israel found themselves in a spiritual dead state. It was the same with Adam and Eve being evicted from the Garden of Eden, they were spiritually dead. Ezekiel said in **Ezekiel 37** that the hand of the Lord came upon him and the Spirit of the Lord set him in the midst of the valley that was full of bones. Bones signify promise- you may be down to skeletal but just one word or one breath from God upon you and you'll be spiritually revived. The valley of dry bones was the spiritual cemetery that represents the spiritual state Israel was in. Their lifestyle caused God to take His Holy presence from them.

Very Many In the Open Valley

Ezekiel 37:2 [2] *Then He caused me to pass by them all around, and behold, there were very many in the open valley; and indeed, they were very dry.* Like the prophet Ezekiel, if a spiritual survey was to be done of the world and many of the organisations that professed to be the "church of Jesus Christ," we will realise their spiritual status. The world we live in doesn't love God and doesn't want anything to do with God. That's why when God came to earth in the form of Jesus Christ they persecuted and rejected Him. **John 15:18-21** [18] *"If the world hates you, you know that it hated Me before it hated you.* [19] *If you were of the world, the world would love its own. Yet because you are not of the world, but I chose you out of the world, therefore the world hates you . . .*

The world rejected the Lord Jesus Christ because they didn't know God. This shows the spiritual state of the world because the world doesn't know God, the world is a spiritual cemetery. It doesn't matter what a person's status is in this world. If they don't know Jesus Christ as Lord and Saviour, they are spiritually dead and need a rebirth. **Ephesians 2:1-2** And you hath he quickened (made spiritually alive), who were dead in trespasses and sins; [2] *In which you formerly walked according to the course of this world, according to the prince of the power of the air, of the spirit that is now working in the sons of disobedience.* **2 Corinthians 4:3-4** [3] But if our gospel be hid, it is hid to them that are lost: [4] In whom the god of this world *has blinded the minds of the unbelieving so that they might not see the light of the gospel of the glory of Christ, who is the image of God.* Satan is the god of this world and it's his spirit that is working in the sons of disobedience in this world. As the god of this world Satan has blinded their minds so that they might not see the light of the gospel of the glory of Christ, who is the image of God. Satan knows that the gospel is the power of God unto salvation (deliverance, freedom). He doesn't want people to be set free from sin. That is the reason he has blinded their eyes that may not know the Truth Who is Jesus Christ. When you are in darkness you are unable to see. Having their eyes blinded makes them spiritually blinded.

The spirit that is in operation in the sons of disobedience is the same spirit that took over Adam and Eve. This spirit causes us to rebel against God's Word. This same spirit is also in operation in many church organisations. Like the scribes and Pharisees whom Jesus describe as being like a grave full of dead men's bones. **Matthew 23:27-28** *[27] Woe unto you, scribes and Pharisees, hypocrites! for ye are like unto whited sepulchres, which indeed appear beautiful outward, but are within full of dead men's bones, and of all uncleanness. [28] Even so ye also outwardly appear righteous unto men, but within ye are full of hypocrisy and iniquity.* Like the scribes and Pharisees who appear righteous, but their inside was like a grave full of dead men's bones. This is the condition of a lot of church organisations. They have an appearance of being righteous but when a spiritual survey is done on them they are like a spiritual cemetery. The reason for this is they don't have a relationship with God and are not connected to Him. They have an appearance of righteousness, but they gravitate to the lust of the flesh and this results in the works of the flesh being evident in their lives no matter how much they want to dress it up by appearing righteous. God said that no flesh will glory in His presence. Religious titles, a position in a church organisation and so-called holy garments doesn't mean much to God when your inside is a spiritual cemetery. God said to the prophet Samuel when he went to anoint David as king over Israel, that man looks at the outward appearance but He God looks at the heart. We can fool man, but we can't fool God.

The prophet Ezekiel said that there were very many in the open valley and they were very dry. The Scriptures reminds us in **Matthew 7**, that wide is the gate, and broad is the way, that leadeth to destruction, and many there be which go in there at: Because strait is the gate, and narrow is the way, which leadeth unto life, and few there be that find it. Israel found themselves in this open valley because of allowing the spirit that operates in the sons of disobedience to operate in them. The result of this was that there were many of them in the open valley and they were dry. From Jesus's teaching in **Matthew 7** we see that there will be many choosing the broad road that leads to destruction. These many, like the many in the open valley, are spiritually dead. The presence of God is absent from their lives, and they are dry. Yes, there is a spiritual drought in their lives. This is one main reason I don't follow the crowd (the many) because not because most people are doing something means it's right or it's pleasing to God. God wants us as His children to be led by His Holy Spirit and have our steps ordered in His Word. Rather than us letting our lives be dictated to by the actions of the many.

Not because most church organisations are doing something means it's right. What does God's Word teach about such practice? When the Apostles were beaten and commanded not to preach in the Name of Jesus anymore, they said they rather obey God than man. Are we going to let the voice of the many drown God's will in our lives? If we allow this to happen, we will find ourselves in an open valley like the many, a state of being spiritually dead. Sad to say this is the state of many church organisations. They gather each week, doing the rituals of men and are operating in a religious spirit instead of being led by the Holy Spirit. The Word of God takes the back seat and the spirit that operates in the sons of disobedience influences them. They then become men pleasers. Their weekly gatherings become a public show. They have all the so-called church moves and the correct church jargon.

Can These Bones Live?

God is such a loving and gracious God whose mercy endures to a thousand generations. Even when we've sinned and messed up badly, He continues to give us chances. That's the love He has for humanity. He says that He doesn't rejoice in the death of a sinner (someone dying in their sins). The question was asked of Ezekiel," Son of man, can these bones live?" He answered, "O Lord God, You know." A true prophet doesn't know everything but only speaks as God reveals because God is the one who knows everything. The church needs to get back to hearing God and not man. Too much flesh, too much lying and false prophets. Too much "Thus saith God," when it wasn't God. Too many leaders manipulate God's people because they believe they are so anointed. God wants His people to be able to discern when it is Spirit and when it is flesh.

As the bones signify promise, we could say God was asking the prophet can these promises live. Even though Israel was spiritually dead, God made a promise to them that if He was hallowed in them He would bring them back to the Promised Land. Wrapped up in those bones were the promises of God's Word. However low in a valley we may find ourselves, it's the promises of God's Word that is going to resurrect us and take us to the mountain top.

Bones are a sign of hope. The hope of God's promise **Genesis 50:25** *25 Then Joseph took an oath from the children of Israel, saying, "God will surely visit you, and you shall carry up my bones from here.* **Exodus 13:19** *19 And Moses took the bones of Joseph with him, for he had placed the children of Israel under solemn oath, saying, "God will surely visit you, and you shall carry up my bones from here with you.* "**Hebrews 11:22** The presence of Joseph's bones among the Israelites was a constant reminder of God's promise to Joseph concerning the promised land. By faith Joseph was able to transcend times by over 400 years. As he was dying, he was able to give instructions that his bones were not to be left in Egypt, but carried into the Promised Land. This was very prophetic and as these words of prophecy were decreed by Joseph, as long as his bones existed those prophetic words were connected to his bones. Not only that but the prophetic words he decreed stayed in the atmosphere for 400 years.

2 Kings 13:21 *21 So it was, as they were burying a man, that suddenly they spied a band of raiders; and they put the man in the tomb of Elisha; and when the man was let down and touched the bones of Elisha, he revived and stood on his feet.* Elijah was one of the most powerful prophets in the Scripture. God worked through him mightily. While he was being raptured up, his mantle fell to Elisha whom he had anointed to be prophet in his stead. God worked through Elisha mightily. However, Elisha's mantle was meant to fall to his servant Gehazi in order for him to continue the prophetic work God started in Elijah. This was not possible because of Gehazi greed and love for money. The lust of the flesh, lust of the eyes and the pride of life got the better of him and he disqualified himself from occupying the prophetic office God had for him. How many people that God has called have missed the mark because of fleshly lust? That's why the scripture said that many are called but few are chosen. In order to attain to the dimension of being chosen by God we must first die to self and the flesh. This will enable us to be able to walk in the Spirit that we will not fulfil the lust of the flesh. Elisha died and the anointing and the mantle he carried was buried with him. Years later only his bones remained in the grave. That anointing that was still in his bones resurrected a dead man who was being buried in Elisha's grave. How many mantles that should have been passed on haven't been passed on because the generation that should have inherited became weak to the flesh? The promise was in the bone, and it brought the dead man back to life.

Prophesy- Hear The Word of The Lord

Ezekiel 37:4 [4] *Again he said unto me, Prophesy upon these bones, and say unto them, O ye dry bones, hear the word of the Lord.* When we prophesy, we speak as God's mouthpiece, God's oracle, we speak God's word. God's word is able to change any situation. There are some demonic influences and happenings occurring now, that God is waiting for His prophets to rise up and speak against. True prophets are anointed to speak into different situations. They can decree a thing and it will be established, as long as it was what God wanted them to decree.

In many church organisations, there are many "thus saith the Lord," when God didn't speak or commanded them to speak. In some church organisations a lying spirit has gone out and camouflaged as it is the Holy Spirit. Prophesying and all sorts but time will reveal that it wasn't God that had spoken. There are many people holding onto false prophecies that they will never see the manifestation of, even to this day. True prophets are chosen from before their mothers' womb. They live a life consecrated, dedicated and pleasing to God. They don't speak when they want to speak but instead speak when they are led to by the Holy Spirit. True prophets speak with the anointing and authority of the Holy Spirit.

As the Lord of Host, everything in creation has the ability to hear when God speaks to it. God commanded the ten plagues to descend on Egypt. He enabled the donkey to speak to its master Balaam after being smitten. He has the ability to let the stones cry out if we fail to praise Him. When Jesus was hungry and came to the fig tree, but no fruit was on it, He commanded the tree not to bear again and the fig tree obeyed Him. There are some unfruitful areas in our lives that just take our valuable resources that we need to speak to. God created the Universe by speaking let there be, and things came into existence. When God restores His Image in us by us being born again in Jesus Christ through water baptism and the infilling of the Holy Spirit, we have the ability to speak life or death to situations because there is life and death in the power of our tongue. The prophet Isaiah tells us that no weapon that is formed against us will be able to prosper and every tongue that rises up against us in judgement we condemn. We condemn these evil tongues that are against us by opening our anointed tongue and reverse every curse and negative words spoken against us.

"O ye dry bones, hear the word of the Lord." No matter how dry up your life may seem, how dry up your situation is there is hope. Tell your dead situation to hear the word of the Lord. Lazarus was dead for four days and stinks. Jesus called him forth from the grave and up from the grave he arose even though he was wrapped in grave clothes. There are areas in our lives that's meant to be fruitful, but they are lying dormant. God wants us to speak to them and call forth fruitfulness again. Some of us are experiencing drought and barrenness in our lives. God wants us to speak to these situations that where there was drought, His rain will start to fall in our lives and the areas that were barren will now bear fruit. Tell your sickness and disease to hear God's word and not the doctors' report, your red seas to part, tell your river Jordan to part, tell your mountain to move, tell them to hear God's word. **Isaiah 41:18** [18] *I will open rivers in high places, and fountains in the midst of the valleys: I will make the wilderness a pool of water, and the dry land springs of water.* **Isaiah 43: 19** [19] *Behold, I will do a new thing; now it shall spring forth; shall ye not know it? I will even make a way in the wilderness, and rivers in the desert.* The God we serve is a miraculous working God. He is able to do what seems impossible to man. He is the Supernatural God. He is able to revive that which was dried up and dead. In Him we live and move and have our being.

God Will Cause His Breath To Enter Into You To Live Again

Ezekiel 37: 5-11 . . . *⁷ So I prophesied as I was commanded: and as I prophesied, there was a noise, and behold a shaking, and the bones came together, bone to his bone. ⁸ And when I beheld, lo, the sinews and the flesh came up upon them, and the skin covered them above: but there was no breath in them. ⁹ Then said he unto me, Prophesy unto the wind, prophesy, son of man, and say to the wind, thus saith the Lord God; Come from the four winds, O breath, and breathe upon these slain, that they may live. ¹⁰ So I prophesied as he commanded me, and the breath came into them, and they lived, and stood up upon their feet, an exceeding great army.*

¹¹ Then he said unto me, Son of man, these bones are the whole house of Israel: behold, they say, our bones are dried, and our hope is lost: we are cut off for our parts.

The state of the dry bones not only represented Israel's spiritual condition but the spiritual condition of people when they are cut off or are separated from God. This was the spiritual state Adam and Eve, and eventually the whole human race that followed, found themselves in after the fall of man. Even though they had flesh and blood on them and life to walk around and do things, when God saw them,

He was looking at a cemetery full of dry bones. This is the state of the world today and those who profess to be a child of God but are hypocrites, a very big cemetery "full of dry bones." **Matthew 23:27-28** *27 Woe unto you, scribes and Pharisees, hypocrites! for ye are like unto whited sepulchres, which indeed appear beautiful outward, but are within full of dead men's bones, and of all uncleanness. 28 Even so ye also outwardly appear righteous unto men, but within ye are full of hypocrisy and iniquity.* This is the true condition of many church organisations. **Revelation 3:14-20** *14 And unto the angel of the church of the Laodiceans write; These things saith the Amen, the faithful and true witness, the beginning of the creation of God; 15 I know thy works, that thou art neither cold nor hot: I would thou wert cold or hot. 16 So then because thou art lukewarm, and neither cold nor hot, I will spue thee out of my mouth. 17 Because thou sayest, I am rich, and increased with goods, and have need of nothing; and knows not that thou art wretched, and miserable, and poor, and blind, and naked: 18 I counsel thee to buy of me gold tried in the fire, that thou mayest be rich; and white raiment, that thou mayest be clothed, and that the shame of thy nakedness do not appear; and anoint thine eyes with eyesalve, that thou mayest see . . .*

Today, the scribes and Pharisees represent the spirit of religion, rituals of man and people who have a form of godliness but living in denial of God's power. Religion and rituals of men don't connect a person to God. Instead, only a genuine relationship that comes only by being born again in Jesus Christ, Who is the Way, Truth and Life can connect us to God. The church of the Laodiceans were rich in material things and had no need of anything. Like some church organisations today, they have their fancy cathedrals, beautiful church buildings, grand synagogues etc. However, in the eyes of the Lord that are in every place beholding the evil and the good, they were wretched, lukewarm, miserable, poor, naked and a very big cemetery of dry bones. Before the eyes of men, they would appear to be all that, but God did a spiritual check, and they were found wanting. That is why God said to Samuel when he went to anoint David as king over Israel, "look not on his countenance, or on the height of his stature; because I have refused him: for the Lord sees not as man sees; for man looks on the outward appearance, but the Lord looks on the heart. Some people are men pleasers and love to put on a show to make those around them smile at any cost but don't care much about what God thinks of them.

Despite all this, God is extending His hand of love and calling people to repentance. He is saying He is rebuking you because He loves you. The son that the father loves he chastises. God is saying trade in the natural for the spiritual, the unholy for the holy in order for Him to provide spiritual covering for your nakedness. God is waiting patiently but He won't wait forever, and He is saying *"Behold, I stand at the door, and knock: if any man hears my voice, and open the door, I will come in to him, and will sup with him, and he with me."* God is seeking and He has provided the opportunity for people to come and have a genuine relationship with Him.

When people repent from their sins and turn to God, like the dry bones He will breathe life anew in us. He will put His Spirit in us and cause us to become spiritually alive and live. The breath God is breathing into us will also cause natural substance to revive and come in place. The sinews are also called tendons (a strong piece of tissue in the body connecting a muscle to a bone). With the sinews or tendons in place the flesh and the skin can take their rightful place. In other words, God is putting back the body together. The body is the house for the soul and the spirit. A reminder that our body is the temple of the Holy Ghost. It is the Spirit of God in us that will cause us to become spiritually quickened and live. Sinews also refer to a part of a structure or system that provides support and holds it together. Somebody is getting ready to live again in Jesus Christ. Your enemies thought you were living life before; God is getting ready to show-off His glory in you. They thought you are going to die but you shall not die but live and declare the works of the Lord. Ezekiel prophesied as he was commanded and there was a noise. The noise is an indication of change, it's an indication of a new season, a new era, and suddenly a rattling; and the bones came together, bone to bone. For three and a half years there was drought and famine in the land of Israel. Elijah said he heard the sound of an abundance of rain and the rain came heavily. God is getting ready to pour out again his Holy Spirit on people if we genuinely repent and turn to Him. Before the manifestation of God's promise there will be a noise or a sound that precedes that manifestation. The bones coming together which are a symbol of promise reminds us of the scripture that says the promises of God are yea and amen. When God speaks, if we do our part, He will do as He has promised.

I Will Open Your Graves

The prophet Ezekiel said as he looked, the sinews and the flesh came upon the dry bones, and the skin covered them over; but *there was* no breath in them. This reminds me of the Creation story in Genesis. The Lord God formed man (man's body) from the dust of the earth. Like Adam's body, the dry bones that were now covered with skin and flesh were lifeless.

Ezekiel was commanded to "prophesy to the breath, and he said to the breath, 'thus says the Lord God: "come from the four winds, O breath, and breathe on these slain, that they may live." So he prophesied as God commanded him, and breath came into them, and they lived, and stood upon their feet, an exceedingly great army. When a true prophet opens his mouth to speak thus saith the Lord, everything in creation has to take heed. He has the anointing to speak life into dead situations and speak to the elements in the earth and the Heavens. Joshua commanded the sun to stand still, it stood still for a day. Elijah prophesied it wouldn't rain for three and a half years and so it did. Here we see Ezekiel prophesying the breath to come from the four winds and the breath obeyed him. Just like in the beginning when God breathed into Adam and he came alive, so the lifeless bodies came alive when the breath came into them. The breath signifies God's Spirit and the lifeless bodies of God's people. When we are filled with the Holy Spirit we are quickened spiritually. Where we didn't have a connection with God, we now have that connection.

As the breath came from the four winds and entered them, they stood upon their feet an exceeding great Army. As children of God we have been enlisted in the army of Jesus Christ. **2 Timothy 2: 3** *³ Thou therefore endure hardness, as a good soldier of Jesus Christ.* As our spirit man becomes alive in Christ, Satan will intensify the war against us. We cannot fight this fight in the flesh but in the Spirit. In the natural armies they fight with natural weapons. However, as the army of Christ we fight spiritual battles. **Ephesians 6:10-13** *¹⁰ Finally, my brethren, be strong in the Lord, and in the power of his might. ¹¹ Put on the whole armour of God, that ye may be able to stand against the wiles of the devil. ¹² For we wrestle not against flesh and blood, but against principalities, against powers, against the rulers of the darkness of this world, against spiritual wickedness in high places. ¹³ Wherefore take unto you the whole armour of God, that ye may be able to withstand in the evil day, and having done all, to stand.* This fight started in Heaven when Lucifer rebelled against God. It's a fight of God against Satan, good against evil, Spirit against flesh. When we are being infilled with the Holy Spirit, we become equipped to fight and be victorious in this war. There are times like Joshua where we must make a righteous stand to be in God's Army. Choose he this day who he will serve but as for me and my house we will serve the Lord. In these End Times God is raising up an army to fight against the Kingdom of Darkness, expose the tricks and devices of Satan and win many souls for the Kingdom of God.

Ezekiel 37: 11-14 . . . *¹³ Then you shall know that I am the Lord, when I have opened your graves, O My people, and*

The Valley Of Dry Bones Experience

brought you up from your graves. [14] *I will put My Spirit in you, and you shall live, and I will place you in your own land. Then you shall know that I, the Lord, have spoken it and performed it," says the Lord.'*

The valley of dry bones represented Israel who are a type of the church. God is getting ready to revive His church, the true church of Jesus Christ. God is getting ready to revive the prodigal sons and daughters. There are many people that God has called, they started the journey of salvation but different circumstances in life have caused them to have fallen by the wayside. Solomon tells us in the book of Proverbs that the righteous man falls several times but he rises again. Like the valley of dry bones, God is getting ready to breathe upon them again. Like the prodigal father, God is there waiting with open arms to see His backslidden children come home. A prerequisite is that they must first come to their rightful mind and realise the life they are living is not what God intended, the place they are now is not what God has ordained for them.

Before the children of Israel stood on their feet like a mighty army, people had written them off, saying their bones were dry and their hope was lost. **Psalm 42:3** [3] *My tears have been my meat day and night, while they continually say unto me, where is thy God?* It's a common thing for unbelievers to question a true child of God faith whenever God is taking us through a process. They tend to question the ability of our God and write us off from society. As we allow God to revive us it should be known that where there was hopelessness, there will now be hope. God is getting ready to revive your health, your marriage, your reproductive system that the enemy has affected, your businesses, your finance, your ministry), The opening of the graves symbolises resurrection and revival. Like Lazarus God is getting ready to call forth His children from grave-like situations. The enemy has designed so many traps against us, with the aim to steal, kill and destroy our lives. Any spiritual graves the enemy have put us in, God Himself is getting ready to open them in order for us to access the promises He has for us. After the graves are open God promises to put His Spirit in us and we shall live. The enemy proposed death and destruction but what the enemy meant for evil God has turned around for our Good. As He put His Spirit in us, we will be able to enter into our own land. That is the position that He has ordained in His Kingdom we will occupy as He intended. Then we will be able to realise that not only has God spoken it but He has also performed it.

CHAPTER 5

Sons And Daughters Of Our Heavenly Father

God Sons in Scripture

A son is a term denoting a male child. It can also be used for a grandson or a more distant descendant. It is also used to denote a foster son and a subject or disciple. Believers in the Lord Jesus Christ are called sons of God. The term sons of God was also a designation for certain godlike beings or angels **(Genesis 6:2-4, Job 1:6, 2:1)**.

The term "son of God" is used in the Hebrew Bible as another way of referring to humans with special relationships with God. In Exodus, the nation of Israel is called God's firstborn son Solomon is also called "son of God". Angels, just and pious men, and the kings of Israel are all called "sons of God."

God had two main sons in Scripture: **Adam** (man-human being)- The last work in the creation of the world.

Adam was formed in God's own image (Genesis 1:26-27). He was made of dust and was brought to life by God breathing into his nostrils the breath of life. (**Genesis 2:7** ... *7 And the LORD God formed man of the dust of the ground (body) and breathed into his nostrils the breath of life (spirit); and man became a living being (soul).* God, who is a Spirit, breathed Himself (Spirit) into Adam's nostrils and he became alive. Before God breathed into Adam of Himself, Adam's body was present, but he didn't come into existence fully until the breath (Spirit) of God entered him. That is why when a person dies, their spirit goes back to God from where it came. **Ecclesiastes 12:7** *7 Then shall the dust return to the earth as it was: and the spirit shall return unto God who gave it.* Based upon Adam's origin the writer of the Gospel of Luke, as he was inspired by the Holy Spirit specifically called Adam a son of God. **Luke 3:38** *38 Which was the son of Enos, which was the son of Seth, which was the son of Adam, which was the son of God.* There is so much wrapped up in this one verse with Adam being called the son of God.

As a son of God who was made in His image and likeness, whatever the image includes, it points to Adam being like the God who created him. While the aspect of infinity would not have been given to a creature, Adam was like God in that he could communicate, in that he could love God's requirements, in that he could express holy affections, in that he could make wise decisions, and in that he could assess situations. He was given authority over all the animals of the earth and lived in the Garden of Eden. Adam was the first man, a living soul in whom all died.

The Lord Jesus Christ (The Second Adam) is referred to as being the Son of God in Scripture. **Matthew 1:18,20** [18] Now the birth of Jesus Christ was on this wise: When as his mother Mary was espoused to Joseph, before they came together, she was found with child of the Holy Ghost. [20] But while he thought on these things, behold, the angel of the LORD appeared unto him in a dream, saying, Joseph, thou son of David, fear not to take unto thee Mary thy wife: for that which is conceived in her is of the Holy Ghost. **Luke 3:21-22** [21] Now when all the people were baptised, it came to pass, that Jesus also being baptised, and praying, the heaven was opened, [22] And the Holy Ghost descended in a bodily shape like a dove upon him, and a voice came from heaven, which said, thou art my beloved Son; in thee I am well pleased.

In nature it takes the seed of a man to fertilise the egg of the woman in order for a child to be produced. With regards to Mary being conceived with Jesus, this wasn't the case. That which was conceived in the Virgin Mary was of the Holy Ghost (God). God, who is a Spirit, put Himself in Mary's womb, resulting in the birth of a baby boy named Jesus. He was also called Emmanuel meaning God is with us. This Jesus was fully God (Son of God-His Divinity) and fully man (Son of Man- His Humanity). The first man Adam who was the son of God came into existence by God forming his body from the dust and breathing His breath (Spirit) into Him. The Second Adam, Jesus Christ was conceived as God who is a Spirit who put Himself into Mary's womb (formed from dust). As the Second or the Last Adam, Jesus Christ was a life-giving spirit in whom all are made alive.

Who Am I? (My Origin, Destiny and Purpose)

I am, and I was a part of history,
My origin, destiny and purpose are no longer a mystery.
The Good Book says man was made in God's image.
At first, I never understood, but then
I realise I'm of a spiritual lineage.
God is a Spirit, and he is truth,
Made in his likeness I have Godly roots.

I am, and I was a part of history,
My origin, destiny and purpose are no longer a mystery.
Man was first spirit, embodied in flesh
He became a living soul.
Formed from the cold clay, there he lay lifeless.
God breathed into him the breath of life,
Acknowledging other living creatures, he began to confess.
I am, and I was a part of history,
My origin, destiny and purpose are no longer a mystery.

Empowered to subdue and have dominion,
Man wasn't good by himself
He was missing a female companion.
He was put to sleep in the first surgical operation.
With the removal of a rib, was formed a woman.
Acknowledging this wonder,
In Holy matrimony two became one.

I am, and I was a part of history,
My origin, destiny and purpose are no longer a mystery.

In their quest for knowledge they were deceived,
No longer were they caretaker of the garden,

Sons And Daughters Of Our Heavenly Father

Of their duty they were relieved.
They no longer had dominion; they were no longer boss.
Plunged into sin they became an outcast.

I am, and I was a part of history
My origin, destiny and purpose are no longer a mystery.

Cast out but not forgotten, because of God's love
They were chastised for their wrong.
Yet before the beginning of time God had a plan
The redemption of man's soul
By sacrificing the Holy Lamb.
No need for a bullock, a dove, or a ram.
Heavenly access through the Second Adam
I'm now able to perform my Godly duty,
Because I'm back in position.
I am, and I was a part of history
My origin, destiny and purpose are no longer a mystery.

My existence is no coincidence,
I was known before my mother's womb.
Born with a sinful nature
Without the shedding of Christ's blood
My life was sure doom.
Redeemed with a price I'm not my own.
Each day hearing his voice another seed is sown.
Rooted and grounded in him I'll abide.
Straight on the narrow not from side to side.
Presenting my body as a living sacrifice,
Afterall my body is the Holy Spirit's temple.
I can't live any and anyhow,
Not like the heathen I've got to be a living example.

I am and I was a part of history
My origin, destiny and purpose are no longer a mystery.

Many are called but I'm chosen and sent,
Not by might I'm on a divine assignment.
Healing, teaching, and feeding the poor,
Rescuing those drowning in sin to salvation's shore.
Entrusted with divine gifts and ability,
Unlike the foolish servant, my talent I'll not bury.
Like the wise and faithful servant, I'll invest wisely,
On the day of harvest, I'll be reaping plenty.
Some thirty, sixty and some a hundredfold,
My reward is more valuable than silver and gold.
I am and I was a part of history
My origin, destiny and purpose are no longer a mystery.

Written 2005. Copyright © 2022.
Richard Scott Brown. All rights reserved.

Power to become the sons of God

St. John 1:10-12 [10] *He was in the world, and the world was made by him, and the world knew him not.* [11] *He came unto his own, and his own received him not.* [12] **But as many as received him, to them gave he power (right, authority, force) to become (reborn) the sons (Children) of God, even to them that believe in his name:** The "He" in this passage is referring to the Lord Jesus Christ. The Bible tells us in Genesis chapter 1 that in the beginning God created the Heavens and the earth. That's right God created the world and not Gods or three Gods. John clearly states that the world was made by Jesus. This means that Jesus Christ was God manifested in flesh. He was in the world that He created and the world (the people in the world) knew Him not. This knowledge speaks of having a personal relationship in order to have knowledge of Him. In order for anyone to know Jesus Christ there must be a Divine revelation. The people in the world are spiritually blind and lack Divine revelation, therefore they didn't know who Jesus Christ was. Today it's not just the world that doesn't know Jesus Christ but we have people in many church organisations professing to be children of God and don't know who Jesus Christ is. We have people teaching and preaching but don't know who Jesus Christ is. People prophesying, leading worship, playing the instruments, serving Holy communion, armour bearing etc but don't know who Jesus Christ is. We have people who are very close to the pastors and the bishops but don't know who Jesus Christ is. We have people being ordained into positions and ministries, but they don't know who Jesus Christ is. There are spouses and children of so-called ministers of the Gospel of Jesus Christ, but they don't know who Jesus Christ is. The world and many church organisations are in a sad state because without the Lord Jesus Christ we will be lost. Our prayers should be "Lord reveal yourself to me." It's going to take a genuine personal relationship with Jesus Christ to truly know who He is. **John 14:9** *Jesus replied, "Have I been with you all this time, Philip, and yet you still don't know who I am? Anyone who has seen me has seen the Father! So why are you asking me to show him to you?* Phillip was around Jesus Christ for many years and witnessed numerous miracles, but he still did not know who Jesus Christ was. It goes to show we can be in God's presence, with all the miracles happening around us but we still don't know who Jesus Christ is.

He came unto His own (The Jews) and they didn't receive (accept) Him. It could be because of the manner He came into this world. Though He was the King of kings and King of the Jews, He was not born in a palace but instead in a manger amongst the animals. Yes, the Most High God, in order to reach mankind became the lowest of the low. Another reason they didn't accept Him was because His teachings dispel their doctrines and rituals of men. They had a form of godliness, but they were denying God's power.

Jesus said that He didn't come to call the righteous but sinners to repentance. In other words He wasn't wasting His time on people who believe they had it all together but yet they've sin and fallen short of God's glory. Jesus's purpose of coming was to call people who recognise they were sinners and fallen short of God's glory, to repentance. Be it Jews or Gentiles. **Romans 11:11, 23** [11] *I say then, have they stumbled that they should fall? God forbid: but rather through their fall salvation is come unto the Gentiles, for to provoke them to jealousy.* [23] *And they also, if they abide not still in unbelief, shall be grafted in: for God is able to graft them in again.* It is through the stumbling and fall of the Jews that a window of opportunity has presented itself for salvation to come unto the Gentiles. God is so good that out of evil comes good. In the process of the Gentiles obtaining salvation, the Jews will be stirred to jealousy and return to God.

John 1:12 [12] *But as many as received him, to them gave he power (right, authority, force) to become (reborn) the sons*

(Children) of God, even to them that believe on his name: Be it Jews or Gentiles, once we received or accept Jesus Christ in our lives He gives us the power to become the sons of God. The word power speaks of having the right or the authority to become a son or a child of God. Having the right or the authority to become a child of God can only be enforced when they are reborn or born again.

Power in physics means the ability to get work done. God has called us to work in His Kingdom. In order for us to successfully and effectively do the works that God has called us to we must first access the power He has made available to us. This power only comes through being baptised with Holy Ghost Power. The harvest is ripe and the labourers are few. It's not necessarily that there are too many lazy Christians but rather Christians who are not equipped with the power that God has made available and they also lack Knowledge. My people are destroyed because of lack of knowledge. Because you have rejected knowledge, I will also reject you as My priests. Since you have forgotten the law of your God, I will also forget your children. The duty of a priest is to offer service and minister before God. The Scripture describes us as being a royal priesthood. In these End Times God is not going to work with ministers who lack knowledge. He said He will also reject us because we have rejected knowledge. That knowledge comes through the study of His Word. The law that they've forgotten symbolises God's Word. The Word of God is the sword of the Spirit. In other words, God is saying He needs people who are available, equipped and have the spiritual knowledge to be His ministers. It is these sons that He is looking for. He has already made available the power that will transform us into this spiritual dimension as His sons. Many church organisations are in a sad state because both leaders and the congregation lack the knowledge that God requires and the lack of this knowledge of God results in God rejecting them. Many are preaching and teaching the Word of God but they lack knowledge of the Word. The reason for this is that they are fleshly and are operating in the flesh. The natural man understands not the things of God because they are spiritually discerned.

Without the Spirit of Christ, we are none of His

Romans 8: 1,5-9 *There is therefore now no condemnation to them which are in Christ Jesus, who walk not after the flesh, but after the Spirit.[5] For they that are after the flesh do mind the things of the flesh; but they that are after the Spirit the things of the Spirit. [6] For to be carnally minded is death; but to be spiritually minded is life and peace. [7] Because the carnal mind is enmity against God: for it is not subject to the law of God, neither indeed can be. [8] So then they that are in the flesh cannot please God. [9] But ye are not in the flesh, but in the Spirit, if so be that the Spirit of God dwell in you. Now if any man has not the Spirit of Christ, he is none of his.* It is a common thing for people to quote "There is no condemnation to those who are in Christ." Yet they leave off the prerequisite of what it takes or what qualifies a person to be in Christ. A lot of preachers do it as well when they don't want to come across as being offensive. I will say it out loud, not everyone who goes to church or who says the Name Jesus is in Christ. To be in Christ you walk after the Spirit and not after the flesh.

It is time we call a spade a spade. Tell people they are wrong when they are wrong, instead of turning a blind eye to their consistent fleshly behaviour because we don't want to lose their membership and with it their tithe and offering.

When you are in Christ no one can condemn you. It doesn't matter your natural circumstances. You may be poor in nature but when you walk in the Spirit you are rich in Christ. Let the weak say I am strong, and the poor say I am rich. When you walk in the Spirit no weapon that is formed against you will be able to prosper and every tongue that rises up against you, you condemn in judgement instead of them condemning you. When you are in Christ you mind the things of the Spirit while a fleshly person will mind the things of the flesh. Let it be known if you are fleshly minded it will only lead to death like Adam and Eve experienced but when you are spiritually minded it will lead to life and peace in Christ. Daily there is a constant war between the flesh and the Spirit. The reason for this is because the fleshly mind is the enemy of God and is not subjected to the law of God and neither can it be. That's why when a person is fleshly they are not in subjection to God's Word and therefore cannot please God.

The harsh reality is this without being born again of the water and the Spirit we don't belong to Christ. It is the Holy Spirit who connects us to Christ and makes us His sons and daughters. If this message was preached more often, more people would seek after and turn to Christ because the reality of life would be correctly presented to them. Instead, we often have some adulterated sugar-coated lies they are professing to be the Gospel of Jesus Christ being preached to people. Without the Spirit of Christ, a person doesn't belong to Him. Another way to put this truth is unless you are born again you are none of Christ. It is having a rebirth that will cause a person to receive the promise of the Father, that is the baptism of the Holy Spirit.

The Sons of God are led by the Holy Spirit

It is by undergoing a spiritual rebirth and being led by the Holy Spirit we become sons of God. Because of this, we have rights and privileges. We have an inheritance in Jesus Christ. This inheritance he willed to us when he was crucified. How much of us who proclaimed to be Christians are not accessing our spiritual inheritance/ our spiritual birthright in Christ? How much of us in the past have accessed it but have sold it like Esau?

Romans 8:14-17 *[14] For as many as are led by the Spirit of God, they are the sons of God. [15] For ye have not received the spirit of bondage again to fear; but ye have received the Spirit of adoption, whereby we cry, Abba, Father. [16] The Spirit itself bears witness with our spirit, that we are the children of God: [17] And if children, then heirs; heirs of God, and joint heirs with Christ; if so be that we suffer with him, that we may be also glorified together.* To be qualified to be a son of God we must be led by the Holy Spirit. In order for us to be led by the Holy Spirit we must be born of the water and of the Spirit. When we are led by the Spirit we die daily to our flesh and submit to the Holy Spirit. Dying daily to our flesh is a process that we must go through in order to come out on the other side like pure gold as sons of God. If we desire to be used effectively by God like the Apostle Paul, we must come to the conclusion that it is no longer I that live but Christ lives in me. **Galatians 2:20** [20] *I am crucified with Christ: nevertheless, I live; yet not I, but Christ lives in me: and the life which I now live in the flesh I live by the faith of the Son of God, who loved me, and gave himself for me.* Like a grain of wheat, the sons of God unless we die to ourselves, we abide alone. However, when we die to self, God produces the anointing in us to be fruitful. It is in the process of repentance and water baptism that we identify with the death, burial, and resurrection of Jesus Christ. In this very important spiritual act, our old man (old sinful nature) is crucified. When we come up out of the water we resurrect as new creatures in Christ. These new creatures are the sons of God. If any man be in Christ, he is a new creature, old things have passed away and all things have become new.

The process of dying to self in order that we can now be led by the Holy Spirit, to become a son of God can be a painful and lonely process. As sons of God, we are not immune from testing and trials. There are unlit crossroads in life that God will lead us down. We have to make the conscious decision, that it is God's way and not my way. When we are being led to the fiery furnace of life and the heat becomes seven times hotter, we must hold fast to our faith in Christ. Just as God proved to His sons in the fiery furnace in Babylon, that if they kept their faith in Him, He would present Himself there with them and they would be unharmed. It is in this manner God wants us to know nowadays that as His sons, He is there with us in every circumstance of our lives.

Acts 14:22 *²² Confirming the souls of the disciples, and exhorting them to continue in the faith, and that we must through much tribulation enter into the kingdom of God.* **Romans 14:17** *¹⁷ For the kingdom of God is not meat and drink; but righteousness, and peace, and joy in the Holy Ghost.* No matter what the Holy Spirit is leading us as sons of God through, as long as our faith in God remains intact we will still be pleasing to God. The many tribulations that we must go through are the keys for us to be able to enter the kingdom of God. The Kingdom of God is not a physical location but a spiritual domain. It's not meat and drink but righteousness, peace and joy in the Holy Ghost. This means the kingdom of God is a spiritual realm we attain to, where, as sons of God, our lives are in subjection to the leading of the Holy Spirit. The result will be righteousness, peace and joy in the Holy Ghost. Righteousness refers to a person being in right standing with God. It is the dying to ourselves and Christ reigning in us as sons of God that put us in right standing with God. The peace and joy in the Holy Ghost refers to the fruit of the Spirit. When we die to ourselves, the works of the flesh will be less evident in our lives and more of the fruit of the Spirit will be seen. The true sons of God are led by the Holy Spirit and the fruit of the Spirit will be evident. **Matthew 7:16-20** *¹⁶ Ye shall know them by their fruits. Do men gather grapes of thorns, or figs of thistles? ¹⁷ Even so every good tree bringeth forth good fruit; but a corrupt tree bringeth forth evil fruit. ¹⁸ A good tree cannot bring forth evil fruit, neither can a corrupt tree bring forth good fruit. ¹⁹ Every tree that bringeth not forth good fruit is hewn down and cast into the fire. ²⁰ Wherefore by their fruits ye shall know them.* We can't fake it to be true sons of God because it is by the fruit of our lives we are known. The lives of the true sons of God will produce good fruits while the lives of people who are not of God will bear evil fruit.

As the Son of God, Jesus Christ was led by the Holy Spirit in the wilderness to be tempted by the Devil while He fasted for forty days. In our time as the sons of God we must be prepared to be led by the Holy Spirit into wilderness experiences where our faith will be tested. It is not just in green pastures that the Holy Spirit will lead us, some of the paths that He'll take us will appear to be like the valley of the shadow of death. The fact that the Holy Spirit is leading us as the sons of God, it means we are not alone and there is no need to fear. The Apostles in the Book of Acts demonstrated this powerfully what it means to live a life where you are led by the Holy Spirit as a son of God. As they preached the Gospel of Jesus Christ, it caused a disturbance in the realm of Hell and a disturbance amongst the Councils, religious leaders (the high priest) and government. They were beaten often not to preach in the Name of Jesus. Like the Hebrew boys they held onto their faith and declared we rather obey God than man. For this they were put in prison but God was with them. Even in the prison the angel of the Lord opened the prison doors and set them free, while commanding them to go and speak in the temple to the people all the words of this life. What amazes me among the group of people who came against the Apostles was the high priest (religious leader). The Scripture said he was filled with indignation (jealousy), because of the numerous miracles the Holy Spirit performed through the Apostles. While people who were sick and bound were being healed and delivered by the power of God, Satan was operating through religious leaders, and they became an offence and a stumbling block to the work of God. It is no different today. Some people are presenting that they are of God in the name of religion and a religious spirit but they have a different agenda. I want to encourage the sons of God who are prepared to be led by the Holy Spirit not to expect smooth sailing all the time but to expect opposition. As we are led by the Holy Spirit we are engaging in Spiritual warfare. However, let us as the sons of God be encouraged that the weapons of our warfare are not carnal (fleshly, natural) but are mighty through God in the pulling down of strong holds.

As the sons of God the tribulations and hardships that we endure enable us to not only die to our flesh but also our will and desires. As Jesus Christ was very close to fulfilling the mandate why He came to earth, that is dying on Calvary Cross in order to redeem the world. He had to battle between the flesh and the Spirit on the Mount of Olives. He prayed and He wrestled within Himself to the point His sweat became like drops of blood. The Spirit eventually overcame the flesh and He was able to say "Father, if thou be willing, remove this cup from me: nevertheless not my will, but thine be done." As Jesus submitted to the will of the Father, flesh subjecting to the Spirit, there appeared an angel unto Him from Heaven, strengthening Him. It is the same when He was tempted in the wilderness and He didn't give in to Satan, angels came and ministered unto Him. The lesson in this for us as sons of God today is that, as we heed the Holy Spirit leading and submit to God's will even in very challenging circumstances, God will send angelic assistance. He proved this with the Apostles in prison when they held onto their faith.

The Holy Spirit will only lead us as the sons of God into God's perfect will for our lives. **In Psalm 37** David wrote that we should delight ourselves also in the Lord: and he shall give us the desires of thine heart. It should be noted God will not give us anything He doesn't desire. What God will give us are the things that He desires for us. Therefore, for us to have God giving us the desires of our heart, we must submit to the Holy Spirit's leading, and our desires will become what God desires for us. **Matthew 7:21-23** [21] *Not everyone that saith unto me, Lord, Lord, shall enter the kingdom of heaven; but he that does the will of my Father which is in heaven.* [22] *Many will say to me in that day, Lord, Lord, have we not prophesied in thy name? and in thy name have cast out devils? and in thy name done many wonderful works?* [23] *And then will I profess unto them, I never knew you: depart from me, ye that work iniquity.* To prove our love for God we must submit to His will and purpose. In the Lord's prayer we are taught to pray "Our Father who art in Heaven. Hallowed be Thy Name, they Kingdom come, they will be done on earth as it is in Heaven." God's will is His Word and what He has commanded us to do. We can be anointed and have the Holy Spirit operating through us performing miracles, prophesying, and casting out devils etc. However, we somehow operated in disobedience and out of God's will for us. This comes down to the motive of our hearts and even though we are anointed by God are we pursuing God's will and seeking to please Him? When the Holy Spirit performs miracles through us, who do we give the glory to? God or ourselves?

The passage above shows us that when we don't do God's will we are working iniquity even though we are anointed. Not only that we can profess to be anointed and God doesn't know us. This means we don't have a genuine relationship with God. It comes back down to the motive of our heart. Our lips can say one thing, but our heart is saying something else. It reminds me of king Saul who was anointed by the prophet Samuel. The will of God for him was to get rid of all the Amalekites and all that they had. He disobeyed God's Word and did what he desired instead. He was anointed but the motive in his heart was different from God's will and commands concerning him. He didn't submit to the leading of the Spirit and this resulted in him being rejected by God and God removing His Spirit from him.

To be a son of God is not just about being anointed, but a true son of God is one who is led by the Holy Spirit and is submitted to the Holy Spirit. Like David, true sons of God are men who are after God's heart, this means we pursue God's will. The Holy Spirit will only lead us in God's will for our lives. How many so-called anointed church leaders are workers of iniquity, yet they are prophesying, working miracles, casting out devils etc? Lucifer was an anointed cherubim in Heaven. Then pride filled him up and iniquity entered his heart. Be warned, so-called anointed church leaders! How many so-called anointed church leaders are not known by God? This means God anoints you initially, but your heart is not after God and neither do you have a relationship with Him. You are pursuing your own glory instead. Be warned! God will not share His glory with another. "For thine is the Kingdom, the power and the glory." King Herod tried to take God's glory for himself when the people called him a god. God's response was to strike him dead with worms eating him alive before the very people who called him a god.

Creation is awaiting the manifestation of the sons of God

Romans 8:16-19 *[16] The Spirit itself bears witness with our spirit, that we are the children of God: [17] And if children, then heirs; heirs of God, and joint-heirs with Christ; if so be that we suffer with him, that we may be also glorified together. [18] For I reckon that the sufferings of this present time are not worthy to be compared with the glory which shall be revealed in us. [19] For the earnest expectation of the creature waits for the manifestation of the sons of God (Young's Literal Translation: For the creation waits with eager longing for the revealing of the sons of God;* **Revised Geneva Translation:** *For the eager expectation of the creation awaits the revealing of the sons of God.).* Despite the spirit of Satan operating in the children of disobedience of this World. Creation is still awaiting in anticipation the manifestation of the sons of God. While the spirit of Satan operates in the children of disobedience of this world, it is the Holy Spirit who will operate in the sons of God. The Holy Spirit will bear witness with our spirit that we are the children of God. We are not just children but heirs and joint-heirs with Christ. This means if we suffer with Christ, we will also be glorified with Him. All that we will endure as good soldiers and children of Christ cannot be compared to the glory that God is going to reveal in us.

The term heirs of God emphasises our relationship with our Heavenly Father. As His children, we have "an inheritance that can never perish, spoil or fade, kept in heaven for us." The Greek term translated "heirs" in **Romans 8:17** refers to "those who receive their allotted possession by right of sonship." In other words, because God has made us His children, we have full rights to receive His inheritance. We are His beneficiaries. Jesus, the only begotten Son of God, is the natural "heir" of the Father. "God said to him, 'You are my Son; today I have become your Father'" Christ's inheritance is the whole universe, all that is in existence: **Hebrews 1:2** says that the Son has been "appointed heir of all things." Being a co-heir with Christ means that we, as God's adopted children, will share in the inheritance of Jesus. What belongs to Jesus will also belong to us. Christ gives us His glory **(John 17:22),** His riches **(2 Corinthians 8:9),** and all things (Hebrews 1:2). We are as welcome in God's family as Jesus is; we are "accepted in the Beloved" **(Ephesians 1:6, NKJV).** All that belongs to Jesus Christ will belong to us, the co-heirs, as well.

"You are no longer a slave, but God's child; and since you are his child, God has made you also an heir" **(Galatians 4:7).** Think of all that means. Everything that God owns belongs to us as well because we belong to Him. Our eternal inheritance as co-heirs with Christ is the result of the amazing grace of God.

There is a glory that God is waiting to pour out in us as His children, at the same time creation is waiting earnestly for our manifestation as the sons of God. For too long Satan and his children of disobedience have gone ahead to influence and take charge. However, God wants us as His children to get in our rightful position in order for us to manifest as his sons. Creation is not just waiting but is crying out for the children of God to come into alignment with God's purpose for our lives. God's Name will and should be glorified. The children of disobedience aren't going to do this. It is us, the children of God who is going to bring Him the glory and honour that is due to His matchless Name. Adam forfeited the authority that God gave him as His son at creation when they fell. When Jesus Christ gave up the ghost on Calvary, He went into Hell and took the keys of death and Hell. In the process He took that which Adam forfeited and has made it available for those who will become His children by being born again of the water and of the Spirit. God is waiting to endue us with His power from a high and show forth His glory in us as He did through the Apostles.

We are living in a time when the children of disobedience are living their lies. They profess their lies as if it is truth, their darkness as if it is light. However, God wants his sons and daughters to arise and shine their light that others will see and come and glorify Him. Like the days of Sodom and Gomorrah the children of disobedience have gone against God's laws and precepts, and no one dear challenged them, or so they think. However, God is waiting for his sons and daughters to arise with His two-edged sword (God's Word) in their mouth and declare God's righteousness upon the earth again. Righteousness exalts a nation, but sin is a reproach to any man.

Like it was in the beginning when the earth was without form and void and gross darkness filled the earth. The Holy Spirit moved upon the face of the earth then God called light into being. We are living in very dark times and gross darkness has filled the earth again but this time with the actions of the children of disobedience of this world. God is getting ready to pour out His Spirit upon His sons and daughters that they may go forth and be the light in this dark world. There are many souls to be won and God doesn't take pleasure in the death of sinners. That's why He is about to raise up sons and daughters to win souls for His Kingdom. **Isaiah 60:1-3** *Arise, shine; For your light has come! and the glory of the Lord is risen upon you.* ² *For behold, the darkness shall cover the earth, and deep darkness the people; But the Lord will arise over you, And His glory will be seen upon you.* ³ *The Gentiles shall come to your light, And kings to the brightness of your rising.* This is a command for the sons of God to arise and shine. For too long we've laid dormant. The Light that came and has come is the Light of the World who is Jesus Christ. He has the Son of Righteousness as the Greater Light. We as His sons and daughters are the lesser lights and like the moon reflects the light of the sun, that's how we ought to reflect the light of Christ and shine bright in this dark world. Not only are we to arise but the glory of the Lord has risen upon us and His glory will be seen in us. That's why creation earnestly awaits our manifestation as the sons of

God. There are many Gentiles (unbelievers) waiting for our manifestation so they can come to the light.

When I think of God's glory the scripture in **2 Chronicles 7 1-3** comes to mind. *Now when Solomon had made an end of praying, the fire came down from heaven, and consumed the burnt offering and the sacrifices; and the glory of the Lord filled the house.* ² *And the priests could not enter into the house of the Lord, because the glory of the Lord had filled the Lord's house.* ³ *And when all the children of Israel saw how the fire came down, and the glory of the Lord upon the house, they bowed themselves with their faces to the ground upon the pavement, and worshipped, and praised the Lord, saying, For he is good; for his mercy endures for ever.* God's glory is a display of His magnificence and this magnificence He wants to manifest in us and through us. A prerequisite for God's glory descending is the effective and fervent prayer by us as His sons. He said if we ask, it shall be given, if we seek we will find and if we knock it shall be opened. When Solomon made an end of praying fire came down from Heaven and the glory of God filled the house. The house or temple that God is interested in is the bodies of his sons and daughters. God wants His glory to fill us (our body is the temple of the Holy Ghost). As the glory of God filled the house the priest couldn't enter. When God's glory descends, flesh can't stand. The people's response was to bow down and worship God. God is seeking to pour out His glory on His sons and daughters that will cause others to submit to Him in true praise and worship.

Thou Mighty Man of Valour

The walls are torn down, the cities lay in waste.
Perverseness has been outspoken; the action of the society has become abased.
Our leaders have become blinded, for too long they've led from the back.
Unstable are their minds, their hands have become slack.
The wrong they have called right; the right they have called wrong.
Surely this isn't of God, He is not the author of confusion.
Brokenness in our homes, instability among the family.
Mothers have to play a dual role; children are raised without a daddy.
Men becoming women, women becoming men, In search of a new identity.
The earth groans for the manifestation of the sons of God.
Women and children have cried, it's time for the men to position themselves
And do their job.

Lest we forget, righteous exalts a nation.
Sin with its reproach has left many in oppression.
Some in mental institutes, many in depression.
High cost of living, economies in recession.
Is there a way out, what is your suggestion?
There are more problems than there are solutions.

The world seems to be facing a global pandemic.
Some people disagree, saying it's a plan-demic.
World leaders are confused, they are getting in a panic.
People are unsure if the cause of this problem is scientific.

Sons And Daughters Of Our Heavenly Father

Where did it all start, the location is not specific.
But those who know their God knows the root is demonic.

Arise and shine for your light has come.
God wants your all, and not just some.
In you, God desires to show forth His glory.
Whatever your past, whatever your story.
He will be that light in you shining in darkness.
While your life becomes a reflection of His goodness.

The battle is waging hot, isn't there a cause?
No more excuses, no more, what if, and but, instead
Be, and because.
It's time to gather pace, for too long you've been on pause.
Arise from your sleep, no more slumber.
Get involved, be a part of the number.

It's time to take the lead and not follow.
Get into the deep, vacate the shallow.
We have a war to fight, some giants to slay.
Please ask someone else, who me? No way
I'm the least among men, my family is poor.
Be it known I'll be with you for sure.
I've entrusted you with Divine Authority, I've given you favour.
Arise, take your rightful place, thou mighty man of valour.

Copyright © 2022 Richard Scott Brown.
All rights reserved. Started writing in 2005,
completed in 2021.

Come out from among them

2 Corinthians 6:14-18 [14] Be ye not unequally yoked together with unbelievers: for what fellowship hath righteousness with unrighteousness? And what communion hath light with darkness? [15] And what concord hath Christ with Belial? Or what part hath he that believeth with an infidel? *For ye are the temple of the living God; as God hath said, I will dwell in them, and walk in them; and I will be their God, and they shall be my people.* [17] *Wherefore come out from among them, and be ye separate, saith the Lord, and touch not the unclean thing; and I will receive you.* [18] *And will be a Father unto you, and ye shall be my sons and daughters, saith the Lord Almighty.*

So, what does the Bible mean by believe? The New Testament Greek word pisteuo (believe) means to "be convinced of something" or "give credence to." We must be convinced that it is an historical fact that more than 2,000 years ago Jesus Christ died on a cross and rose on the third day.

Being convinced of those facts, however, is not enough. One must accept or personally appropriate them as being true. Note that we are not merely accepting as true that He died and arose. We are acknowledging that He did it for us. In a substitutionary "instead of us" death, Christ died in our place. The punishment we deserve, He suffered for us. Christ saved us by dying for us. The third day He arose, proving that as God He conquered both sin and death.

The word believe also means to have a firm persuasion of anything. That means when opposition comes one will not be persuaded otherwise.

A believer then is one who has been instructed in the truths of the gospel and is baptised. **Acts 8:12** *[12] But when they believed Philip preaching the things concerning the kingdom of God, and the name of Jesus Christ, they were baptised, both men and women. **Acts 16:31-33** [31] And they said, believe on the Lord Jesus Christ, and thou shalt be saved, and thy house. [32] And they spake unto him the word of the Lord, and to all that were in his house. [33] And he took them the same hour of the night, and washed their stripes; and was baptised, he and all his, straightway.* **James 2:21-24** *[21] Was not Abraham our father justified by works when he offered Isaac his son on the altar? [22] Do you see that faith was working together with his works, and by works faith was made perfect? [23] And the Scripture was fulfilled which says, "Abraham believed God, and it was accounted to him for righteousness." And he was called the friend of God. [24] You see then that a man is justified by works, and not by faith only.*

According to the book of James when we say we believe, God expects us to back it up with action. It's the same when we say we are believers of the Gospel of Jesus Christ we must put this into action by first repenting of our sins, then obey the command to be water baptised in the Name of Jesus Christ for the remission of our sins. After this we will receive the baptism of the Holy Spirit. We see these facts being demonstrated in the Scriptures posted above from the Book of Acts. In Acts 8, after Phillip preached the Kingdom of God and the Name of Jesus Christ, both men and women believed and were baptised. In Acts chapter 16 the troubled prison guard asked the question "what must I do to be saved?" Paul replied believe in the Lord Jesus Christ and you shall be saved. The Scripture goes on to say, they speak the word of the Lord to Him. Remember faith comes by hearing and hearing the word of the Lord. However, faith without works is dead work. The prison guard and his household put their faith into action by obeying the command to be water baptised, this was done by the Apostles.

I want to silence this false notion that a person is a believer because they just "hear the Gospel", "say a so-called sinner's prayer" and continue to live a life of sin. Or a person is a believer because they attend a church organisation. Even devils, witches and freemasons go to church organisations. In **2 Corinthians 6** the command is that a believer should not be unequally yoked together with unbelievers. After that various thought-provoking questions were posed. What fellowship hath righteousness with unrighteousness? What communion hath light with darkness? What concord (agreement) hath Christ with Belial? Or what part hath he that believeth with an infidel? What agreement hath the temple of God with idols? In the book of 1 Peter, we are commanded to be holy as the Lord God is Holy. **Hebrews 12:14** [14] *Follow peace with all men, and holiness, without which no man shall see the Lord.* The verse in Hebrews is basically telling us that without a life of holiness our soul will be lost. This just dropped in my spirit as I'm typing. There is a difference between righteousness and holiness. Righteousness means to be in right standing with God because of the redemptive work of the Lord Jesus Christ on Calvary's Cross over 2000 years ago. While holiness is the lifestyle that we will live to maintain that right standing with God. As sons and daughters of God we are clothed with the characteristics of holiness. Living a lifestyle of holiness will cause us to draw near to God and He will draw near to us, at the same time resisting the Devil and he will flee from us.

As sons and daughters of our Heavenly Father God wants us to recognise that our bodies are the temple of the Holy Ghost. A temple is a place of worship. Worship is paying homage (tribute, honour, respect, reverence, praise) to God for who He is. Worship is the adoration and glorification of God by those who have been made new creatures in Christ. True worship is the greatest way we can show our love for God. Worship implies "worth-ship." We worship and praise God because He is worthy of our praise. The scripture goes on to say, God has said, He will dwell in us, and walk in us; and He will be our God, and we shall be His people. This is very powerful. Many years ago people would pilgrimage to Jerusalem to offer worship. However, God is saying to us today, that's not necessary. Instead, when we become born again of the water and the Holy Spirit, as His sons and daughters, we have His indwelling Presence. To the extent every step we take He'll be there walking in us. That means we can offer true worship to God twenty-four hours per day. This means God is near to us, as the sons and daughters of our Heavenly Father we are God carriers, hallelujah. We carry the Holy presence of God in us. This is a selah moment. If you are truly born again, you have the Creator of this Universe dwelling and walking in you. This also means there is no room for Satan and his demons.

There is a prerequisite for all of this to happen. We are commanded in **2 Corinthians 6:17-18** *17 Wherefore come out from among them, and be ye separate, saith the Lord, and touch not the unclean thing; and I will receive you.18 And I will be a Father unto you, and ye shall be my sons and daughters, saith the Lord Almighty.* In order for us to be qualified to have the Creator of this Universe dwelling and walking us we need to come out from among darkness, unbelievers, idols, etc. God wants us to put away the cigarette, marijuana and the lighter and let Christ shine His light in us. Put away the garments of prostitution and be clothed in righteousness and holiness. No more coke and cocaine and become high in His presence. Away with the alcohol and other spirits and be filled with the Holy Spirit. Come out of your life of mess and pursue the Gospel message. When we obey these commands then we are qualified to be called sons and daughters of our Heavenly Father. Let me boldly say this. We are all God's creation, but we are not all His children. To be called a child of God or a son and a daughter of our Heavenly Father we must have His DNA. God is a Spirit, and His DNA is His Holy Spirit. To inherit this DNA, we must be born again of the water and the Spirit. Romans 8 tells us that those who are led by the Spirit are the sons of God. **Galatians 4:4-7** *4 But when the fulness of the time was come, God sent forth his Son, made of a woman, made under the law, 5 To redeem them that were under the law, that we might receive the adoption of sons. 6*

And because ye are sons, God hath sent forth the Spirit of his Son into your hearts, crying, Abba, Father. ⁷ *Wherefore thou art no more a servant, but a son; and if a son, then an heir of God through Christ.*

As qualified sons and daughters of our Heavenly Father God wants us to remember that **1 Peter 2:9-10** ⁹ *But ye are a chosen generation, a royal priesthood, an holy nation, a peculiar people; that ye should show forth the praises of him who hath called you out of darkness into his marvellous light;* ¹⁰ *Which in time past were not a people, but are now the people of God: which had not obtained mercy, but now have obtained mercy.* It should be mentioned that as sons and daughters of our Heavenly Father we are no ordinary people. Firstly, we are a chosen generation. What makes us chosen is because we have made the choice to answer the call of God in our lives. Many are called but few are chosen. We are a royal priesthood because our Heavenly Father is the King of kings. Because the King of kings dwells and walks in us we can now decree a thing and it shall be established. Seeing that life and death lies in the power of our tongue. We are a holy nation and a peculiar people. Therefore, holiness must be the order of the day. We are a peculiar people which before were not a people. God has chosen us as His sons and daughters to show forth His praise. These people have I formed for myself that they may show forth my praise. We ought to live a life that will bring glory and honour to God.

When you hear the word "father," do you think of someone who is loving...or angry? Someone who is pleased with you . . . or constantly disappointed? Someone who is always available . . . or someone who is too busy, preoccupied, or distant? When you think of "Father God," what images come to mind?

Regardless of the type of father you grew up with—or without—it is likely that your view of God is influenced by the relationship you had with your father. The characteristics of a good father are as follows. A good father makes provision for his family. He also offers protection, and he is loving, kind, caring and gives guidance to his children.

Our Heavenly Father is all of these to us and more. **Matt 7:7-11** [7] *Ask, and it shall be given you; seek, and ye shall find; knock, and it shall be opened unto you:* [8] *For every one that ask receives; and he that seeks finds; and to him that knocks it shall be opened.* [9] *Or what man is there of you, whom if his son ask bread, will he give him a stone?* [10] *Or if he ask a fish, will he give him a serpent?* [11] *If ye then, being evil, know how to give good gifts unto your children, how much more shall your Father which is in heaven give good things to them that ask him*

CHAPTER 6

I Will Pour Out My Spirit Unto You

The promise of the Holy Spirit in Joel

Joel 2:1-2,10-15, 23-32 *Blow ye the trumpet in Zion, and sound an alarm in my holy mountain: let all the inhabitants of the land tremble: for the day of the Lord cometh, for it is nigh at hand;* [2] *A day of darkness and of gloominess, a day of clouds and of thick darkness, as the morning spread upon the mountains: a great people and a strong; there hath not been ever the like, neither shall be any more after it, even to the years of many generations.* [10] *The earth shall quake before them; the heavens shall tremble: the sun and the moon shall be dark, and the stars shall withdraw their shining:* [11] *And the Lord shall utter his voice before his army: for his camp is very great: for he is strong that executes his word: for the day of the Lord is great and very terrible; and who can abide it?* [12] *Therefore also now, saith the Lord, turn ye even to me with all your heart, and with fasting, and with weeping, and with mourning . . .*

²⁵ And I will restore to you the years that the locust hath eaten, the cankerworm, and the caterpillar, and the palmerworm, my great army which I sent among you . . .

²⁸ And it shall come to pass afterward, that I will pour out my spirit upon all flesh; and your sons and your daughters shall prophesy, your old men shall dream dreams, your young men shall see visions: ²⁹ And also upon the servants and upon the handmaids in those days will I pour out my spirit. ³⁰ And I will show wonders in the heavens and in the earth, blood, and fire, and pillars of smoke. ³¹ The sun shall be turned into darkness, and the moon into blood, before the great and terrible day of the Lord come. ³² And it shall come to pass, that whosoever shall call on the name of the Lord shall be delivered: for in mount Zion and in Jerusalem shall be deliverance, as the Lord hath said, and in the remnant whom the Lord shall call.

Joel is referred to as one of the Minor prophets. Minor in the sense of the volume of what is written. To understand the prophets, we must know the historical setting of their prophecies. Their messages were delivered for the time in which they lived. While predictions concerned future times, they had a vital bearing upon the people to whom they were spoken. A judgement predicted may not be visited upon them for years to come, but the conduct of the people who hear the message are responsible for that judgement. It is for them to save the nation from such a calamity. The prophet speaks from the standpoint of existing conditions, as well as from the standpoint of predictions fulfilled.

Following the reign of king Jehoshaphat, Judah rapidly declined as the good effects of that king's reformation disappeared in the apostasy of his son Jehoram, who married Athaliah, the daughter of Ahab and Jezebel of Israel. Judah was plunged into iniquity which continued until the time of Hezekiah. How often have we seen the hard work of an individual/s easily go up in smoke because of the folly of the leaders that succeed them. Jehoshaphat was a righteous king but his son Jehoram was evil. It was this state of things in which Joel lived and it was to a people hardened in sin that he spoke the judgments of Jehovah. It was at this time that Judah was visited by a plague of a most devastating nature. The land was covered with swarms of locusts that destroyed vegetation. Added to this was a drought and the people faced starvation.

Joel chapter 2 opens with an urgent warning about the Day of the Lord which was near at hand. The Day of the Lord is a day inaugurating the eternal universal rule of God. In the Old Testament, an eschatological day of ultimate judgement bringing final deliverance or doom -also called day of Yahweh. In the New Testament, the triumphant day of Christ's return to earth in glory. As we read this passage it outlines some of the events that will occur when the Day of the Lord comes.

The Old Testament passages dealing with the day of the Lord often convey a sense of imminence, nearness, and expectation: "Wail, for the day of the Lord is near!" **(Isaiah 13:6)**; "For the day is near, even the day of the Lord is near" **(Ezekiel 30:3)**; "Let all who live in the land tremble, for the day of the Lord is coming. It is close at hand" **(Joel 2:1)**; "Multitudes, multitudes in the valley of decision! For the day of the Lord is near in the valley of decision" **(Joel 3:14)**; "Be silent before the Lord God! For the day of the Lord is near" **(Zephaniah 1:7)**. This is because the Old Testament passages referring to the day of the Lord often speak of both a near and afar fulfilment, as does much of Old Testament prophecy. Some Old Testament passages that refer to the day of the Lord describe historical judgements that have already been fulfilled in some, while others refer to divine judgments that will take place toward the end of the age.

The New Testament calls it a day of "wrath," a day of "visitation," and the "great day of God Almighty" **(Revelation 16:14)** and refers to a still future fulfilment when God's wrath is poured out on unbelieving Israel and on the unbelieving world. The Scriptures indicate that "the day of the Lord" will come quickly, like a thief in the night **(Zephaniah 1:14-15; 2 Thessalonians 2:2),** and therefore Christians must be watchful and ready for the coming of Christ at any moment.

After an outline of the events of God's judgement, the people were called into repentance from their evil acts. A demonstration of them going into repentance included rending their heart and not their garments, fasting and prayer. If the people genuinely turned to God, He promised to restore the things they lost in nature by the way of God's mighty army (locust, cankerworm, caterpillar and palmerworm) that he sent to afflict them. God is not just a God of judgement, but He is a loving and a God of restoration. God had promised to restore the oil, wine and the corn after many years of famine and drought. During the reign of Jehoshaphat, the people experienced plenty because he was a righteous king who led the people to worship God. Because of this when they went into battle God granted them the victory and they were rewarded with the spoils of the enemy. On the other hand, Jehoram who succeeded Jehoshaphat had the influence of the Jezebel spirit that shed the blood of his brethren. He also strengthened himself. In all of this he worked evil in God's eyes by setting up high places (idolatry) in the mountain of Judah and causing the inhabitants of Jerusalem to commit fornication.

Jehoram's leadership is symbolic of some leaders of church organisations today. They are only there to establish themselves and their family. Judah means praise, and it was in the mountain of Judah (praise) Jehoram set up the high places. That means he corrupted the true praises of God and turned it into idolatry. Unlike his father Jehoshaphat who led by example and worshipped God with the people following likewise. Where the praise and worship were evident, God granted victory with an abundance of the enemies' spoils. In Jehoram's reign idolatry and sexual immorality were evident and hence the judgement of God was meted out to them.

In calling the people to repentance, we see where God called for the leaders (priests and ministers of the Lord) to take the fore-front and lead by example. It was corrupt leaders that led the people's heart away from God and therefore it will be righteous leaders that will lead the people's heart back to God. God promised that as the leaders led the people into repentance that He would respond to their cry of repentance and send them corn, wine and the oil. In all of this God promised that they would be satisfied and no longer be a reproach to the nations. Corn represents the increase and blessings of the harvest. Wine represents the revelation of God's Spirit filled Word and oil represents the anointing of the Holy Spirit upon God's Word. When we genuinely turn to God He will bless us threefold with the natural resources including health, in addition to the revelation of His word and the outpouring of His anointing.

Genuine repentance also moves God's heart to turn from the judgement that people deserved because of their evil actions. We see this in the book of Jonah, when Jonah warned the people to repent and fast. Their obedience stops God's judgement from being poured out on them. This is a perfect example for us today. If we turn from our fleshly ways and seek God, He will restore us.

This genuine repentance by the children of Israel not only resulted in restoration of material things but there was a sudden change in the tone of the prophet. Joel prophesied **Joel 2:28-29** *And it shall come to pass afterward, that I will pour out my spirit upon all flesh; and your sons and your daughters shall prophesy, your old men shall dream dreams, your young men shall see visions:* [29] *And also upon the servants and upon the handmaids in those days will I pour out my spirit.* God wants us as His people to realise that he cares about our physical needs but even more so our spiritual needs. Man shall not live by bread alone but by every word that proceeds out of God's mouth. Bread is to sustain the body while God's word which is Spirit and life is to sustain our soul and spirit. This promise of God's outpouring speaks of a spiritual revival. All the years Israel was in apostasy the people were like the valley of dry bones, they were spiritually dead. This promise had an even greater significance, that is future revivals which were not just limited to the Day of Pentecost. Jonah did not just predict Pentecost, but he predicts the outpouring of God's Spirit and if any future outpouring was to take place, we should consider it a fulfilment of this prophecy.

This prophecy of God's outpouring was sandwiched between restoration in nature and events of the Day of the Lord. Even then, there was a ray of hope. The scripture said after these events that it shall come to pass, that whosoever shall call on the name of the Lord shall be delivered: for in mount Zion and in Jerusalem shall be deliverance, as the Lord hath said, and in the remnant whom the Lord shall call. That word calls on means to invoke. In water baptism we call on or invoke the Name of the Lord Jesus Christ for the remission of sins. The Scripture teaches us that there is no other Name given under Heaven or earth by which we must be saved. There is an awesome power when we call on or invoke the Name of Jesus. Principalities and powers recognise this great Name.

The promise of the Holy Spirit in Proverbs

Proverbs 1:22-29 [22] *How long, ye simple ones, will ye love simplicity? and the scorners delight in their scorning, and fools hate knowledge?* [23] *Turn (repent) you at my reproof (rebuke, correction): behold, I will pour out my spirit unto you, I will* make known my words unto you. *²⁴ Because I have called, and ye refused; I have stretched out my hand, and no man regarded; ²⁵ But ye have set at nought all my counsel and would none of my reproof: ²⁶ I also will laugh at your calamity; I will mock when your fear cometh; ²⁷ When your fear cometh as desolation, and your destruction cometh as a whirlwind; when distress and anguish cometh upon you. ²⁸ Then shall they call upon me, but I will not answer; they shall seek me early, but they shall not find me: ²⁹ For that they hated knowledge and did not choose the fear of the Lord: ³⁰ They would none of my counsel: they despised all my reproof.*

The writings of the book of Proverbs which is attributed to king Solomon, were written almost 200 years before the book of Joel. The book of Proverbs relates to wisdom that is applicable for daily living. However, as I read the 1st chapter of Proverbs, I came across something very prophetic in verse 23. *²³ Turn (repent) you at my reproof (rebuke, correction): behold, I will pour out my spirit unto you, I will make known my words unto you.* Over the years This verse has ministered to me so much. As I analyse this verse, it draws similarity in some ways with the prophecy that was spoken in Joel chapter 2 about the outpouring of God's Spirit. God not only promises to pour out His Spirit in Proverbs but also to make known His words. This is a powerful two-fold blessing that is being promised.

As in the book of Joel, preceding the promise of the outpouring of God's Spirit is the call to repentance. The priests and the ministers were called to take the lead in bringing the people into repentance back to God. Throughout Scripture we see when people repent God would grant them His love, mercy, forgiveness, and grace. This shows how much God genuinely loves people.

The word *repentance* in the Bible literally means "the act of changing one's mind," by turning away from a life of sin and turning to God. Repentance is being convicted in your heart of the wrongs you have done and you are willing to make a change. To repent and to convert involved obedience to God's revealed will, placing trust in him, turning away from all evil and ungodliness. Each person was to «turn from his wicked evil way» **(Jer 26:3; 36:3).** In the Old Testament, repentance, or wholehearted turning to God, is a recurring theme in the message of the prophets. Repentance was demonstrated through rituals such as fasting, wearing sackcloth, sitting in ashes, wailing, and liturgical laments that expressed strong sorrow for sin. These rituals were supposed to be accompanied by authentic repentance, which involved a commitment to a renewed relationship with God, a walk of obedience to His Word, and right living. Often, however, these rituals merely represented remorse and a desire to escape the consequences of sin.

Repentance was the message that the Lord Jesus Christ and the prophet John the Baptist preached, when they began their ministry. **Luke 5:31-32** [31] *And Jesus answering said unto them, they that are whole need not a physician; but they that are sick.* [32] *I came not to call the righteous, but sinners to repentance.* This verse emphasises God's love for mankind, in that if we genuinely turn to Him, He will reciprocate this by turning to us by forgiving our sins. In order for a person to experience God's forgiveness they must first realise like a sick person; they need the help of a doctor. Likewise, a sinner realising they are indeed of God's mercy. It's very important for individuals to be able to acknowledge their wrongs. Afterall, we have all sinned and come short of God's glory.

When we heed the call to repentance, we will experience God's goodness. However, if we continue to walk in disobedience to God's commands, we will experience His wrath. Noah preached for decades calling the people to repentance. However, no one heeded the call except Noah's household. Whatever the size of the population in that era was, sadly only eight souls were spared God's judgement and were saved in the Ark. In **Proverbs 1** God gave the call of repentance and He promises to pour out His Spirit and make known His word. Before repentance, we were going our own way and living a life being led by the flesh.

However, when we repent, our steps become ordered in God's word, we pursue God's will and we receive the outpouring of God's Spirit. **Psalm 119** declares how a young man cleanse his way but by taking heed to God's word. That's the reason God promises if we turn when He rebukes us not only will He pour out His Spirit, but He will make known His word to us. Receiving an outpouring of God's Spirit is only a part of what God promises us. The Holy Spirit is there to lead us into God's will. Jesus promises us that when the Comforter (Holy Spirit) comes He will lead us into all truth. The Scripture tells us that God's word is truth. The Holy Spirit is there to make known God's word to us because the natural man cannot understand the things of God because they are spiritually discerned. There must be a balance of the Holy Spirit and the word of God in a believer's life. The Holy Spirit without God's word or God's word without the Holy Spirit in a believer's life results in Spiritual deficiency. The word of God is the sword of the Holy Spirit. If we are to truly walk in spiritual authority as sons and daughters of our Heavenly Father, we must experience the outpouring of God's Spirit and having God making known His word to us.

There is a flip side to those who don't repent when God tells them to. **Proverbs 1:24-31** *[24] Because I have called, and ye refused; I have stretched out my hand, and no man regarded; [25] But ye have set at nought all my counsel and would none of my reproof: [26] I also will laugh at your calamity; I will mock when your fear cometh; [27] When your fear cometh as desolation, and your destruction cometh as a whirlwind; when distress and anguish cometh upon you. [28] Then shall they call upon me, but I will not answer; they shall seek me early, but they shall not find me: [29] For that they hated knowledge and did not choose the fear of the Lord: [30] They would none of my counsel: they despised all my reproof. [31] Therefore shall they eat of the fruit of their own way and be filled with their own devices.* Solomon spoke as God's prophet and made it clear that just like the disobedient people in Noah's days, if we continue in disobedience, we are going to experience God's judgement.

Day of Pentecost

Acts 2:1-21 *[1] And when the day of Pentecost was fully come, they were all with one accord in one place. [2] And suddenly there came a sound from heaven as of a rushing mighty wind, and it filled all the house where they were sitting. [3] And there* *appeared unto them cloven tongues like as of fire, and it sat upon each of them.* ⁴ *And they were all filled with the Holy Ghost, and began to speak with other tongues, as the Spirit gave them utterance.*

⁵ *And there were dwelling at Jerusalem Jews, devout men, out of every nation under heaven.* ⁶ *Now when this was noised abroad, the multitude came together, and were confounded, because that every man heard them speak in his own language.* ⁷ *And they were all amazed and marvelled, saying one to another, Behold, are not all these which speak Galileans?* ⁸ *And how hear we every man in our own tongue, wherein we were born?* ⁹ *Parthians, and Medes, and Elamites, and the dwellers in Mesopotamia, and in Judaea, and Cappadocia, in Pontus, and Asia,* ¹⁰ *Phrygia, and Pamphylia, in Egypt, and in the parts of Libya about Cyrene, and strangers of Rome, Jews and proselytes,*

¹¹ *Cretes and Arabians, we do hear them speak in our tongues the wonderful works of God.* ¹² *And they were all amazed, and were in doubt, saying one to another, What meant this?* ¹³ *Others mocking said, these men are full of new wine.* ¹⁴ *But Peter, standing up with the eleven, lifted up his voice, and said unto them, Ye men of Judaea, and all ye that dwell at Jerusalem, be this known unto you, and hearken to my words:* ¹⁵ *For these are not drunken, as ye suppose, seeing it is but the third hour of the day.* ¹⁶ *But this is that which was spoken by the prophet Joel.* ¹⁷ *And it shall come to pass in the last days, saith God, I will pour out of my Spirit upon all flesh: and your sons and your daughters shall prophesy, and your young men shall see visions, and your old men shall dream dreams:* ¹⁸ *And on my servants and on my handmaidens I will*

pour out in those days of my Spirit; and they shall prophesy: [19] *And I will show wonders in heaven above, and signs in the earth beneath; blood, and fire, and vapour of smoke:* [20] *The sun shall be turned into darkness, and the moon into blood, before the great and notable day of the Lord come:* [21] *And it shall come to pass, that whosoever shall call on the name of the Lord shall be saved.*

The historical and Biblical origins of what we know as Pentecost today can be found in **Exodus 23:14-19**, **Leviticus 23:15-16** and **Deuteronomy 16:10.** One of three significant Jewish festivals, Pentecost is the Greek name for the Festival of Weeks, a prominent feast in the Jewish calendar that celebrates God giving them the Ten Commandments fifty days after the Exodus from Egypt. God instructed his people to celebrate the Festival of Weeks, which was to be held seven full weeks (49 days) plus one day after Passover (Jesus Christ became our Passover when He was crucified on Calvary's Cross), equalling fifty days. Also called the Feast of Harvest, this was when the Jews would present offerings of the first fruits of their spring crops. Jewish law required all adult Jewish men to come to Jerusalem from wherever they were living to personally be in attendance for the celebration.

This is the context in which **Acts 2** begins, saying "When the day of Pentecost came ... there were staying in Jerusalem God-fearing Jews from every nation under heaven ... Parthians, Medes, Elamites, residents of Mesopotamia, Judea, Cappadocia, Pontus, Asia, Phrygia, Pamphylia, Egypt, Libya and Rome, Cretans and Arabs" **(Acts 2:1, 5, 9-11).** When the Holy Spirit arrived on the Day of Pentecost, it was to symbolise that it was the new first fruit of God's spiritual harvest to come, the second coming of Jesus and redemption of his Church.

Pentecost was the celebration of the beginning of the early weeks of harvest. In Palestine, there were two harvests each year. The early harvest came during the months of May and June; the final harvest came in the Fall. Pentecost was the celebration of the beginning of the early wheat harvest, which meant that Pentecost always fell sometime during the middle of the month of May or sometimes in early June.

Prior to the outpouring of the Holy Spirit, Jesus commanded the Apostles that they should not depart from Jerusalem, but wait for the promise of the Father, which they have heard of Him. He reminded them that John truly baptised with water; but they shall be baptised with the Holy Ghost not many days hence. He told them they shall receive power, after that the Holy Ghost will come upon them. The purpose of this power was so they should be witnesses unto Him both in Jerusalem, and in all Judaea, and in Samaria, and unto the uttermost part of the earth. Peter explained that them being a witness of Jesus Christ was to be a witness of His Resurrection from the grave. These were the last words Jesus spoke before His Ascension. The apostles being a part of the one hundred and twenty, all continued with one accord in prayer and supplication. This included the women, and Mary the mother of Jesus, and with his brethren.

In walking in obedience to the Lord Jesus's command. Two things were evident as the one hundred and twenty sought God for the outpouring of His Holy Spirit. Firstly,

I Will Pour Out My Spirit Unto You

they continued in one accord and secondly in prayer and supplication. If we are going to experience a great outpouring of God in these end times, we must all be in one accord. That is to be in and remain in unity. **Psalm 133:1-3** *Behold, how good and how pleasant it is for brethren to dwell together in unity!* ² *It is like the precious ointment upon the head, that ran down upon the beard, even Aaron's beard: that went down to the skirts of his garments.* ³ *As the dew of Hermon, and as the dew that descended upon the mountains of Zion: for there the Lord commanded the blessing, even life forevermore.* It is in the atmosphere of unity and one accord God commands His blessings. The blessing in this instance is the outpouring of God's Spirit.

The one hundred and twenty continued in one accord with prayers and supplication. A prayer of supplication is seeking for God's will. We come to God in prayer for a variety of reasons—to worship Him, to confess our sins and ask for forgiveness, to thank Him for His blessings, to ask for things for ourselves, and/or to pray for the needs of others. The Hebrew and Greek words most often translated "supplication" in the Bible mean literally "a request or petition," so a prayer of supplication is asking God for something. Unlike the prayer of petition, which is praying on behalf of others, the prayer of supplication is generally a request for the person praying. Daniel set us an example in **Daniel 9:3** ³ *And I set my face unto the Lord God, to seek by prayer and supplications, with fasting, and sackcloth, and ashes.* It is possible the one hundred and twenty in the Upper Room were not just in prayer and supplication but at the same time were seeking in fasting as well. When we pray, we communicate with God to have His will be done in our lives but when we fast we are putting the flesh under subjection in order for God to empower us with His Holy Spirit.

It was significant that they were gathered in the Upper room. **1 Kings 17: 17-21** [17] *Now it happened after these things that the son of the woman who owned the house became sick. And his sickness was so serious that there was no breath left in him.* [18] *So she said to Elijah, "What have I to do with you, O man of God? Have you come to me to bring my sin to remembrance, and to kill my son?"* [19] *And he said to her, "Give me your son."* *So, he took him out of her arms and carried him to the upper room where he was staying, and laid him on his own bed.* [20] *Then he cried out to the Lord* and said, "O *Lord* my God, have You also brought tragedy on the widow with whom I lodge, by killing her son?" [21] *And he stretched himself out on the child three times, and cried out to the Lord* and said, "O *Lord* my God, I pray, let this child's soul come back to him." [22] *Then the Lord* heard the voice of Elijah; and the soul of the *child came back to him, and he revived.* Here we see the widow's son dying. Elijah took him to the "Upper Room". In the "Upper Room" Elijah prayed and sought God asking for the child's soul to come back to him. Then the Lord heard the voice of Elijah and the child was revived. Like the Upper Room in **Acts 2**, this "Upper Room" in **1 Kings 17** represents a place of revival but preceding revival was prayer and supplication in both Upper Rooms. In the Upper Room flesh must die, the will of man must die, then God will pour out of His Spirit. In the Upper Room God will get the glory because the natural is transformed by the Supernatural, what was dead becomes alive. In the Upper Room what God promised comes into manifestation. For thine is the kingdom, power and the glory.

When the Day of Pentecost was fully come, they were all in one accord in one place. And suddenly there came a sound from heaven as of a rushing mighty wind, and it filled all the house where they were sitting. And there appeared unto them cloven tongues like as of fire, and it sat upon each of them. And they were all filled with the Holy Ghost, and began to speak with other tongues, as the Spirit gave them utterance. The outpouring of the Holy Spirit is God fulfilling His promise as the prophet Joel spoke hundreds of years before. God is not a man that He should lie. When we are united according to God's will and word, the environment becomes conducive for a great outpouring and revival. We must be in agreement to what is written in God's word. Notice the Holy Spirit gave them utterance and they spoke with other tongues.

When we are filled with the Holy Spirit, we have the Kingdom of God living in us. When a person is a citizen in a particular Kingdom, they speak the language of that Kingdom. The outpouring of the Holy Spirit on the one hundred and twenty was at a time where the people gathered on the outside to celebrate the Feast of Weeks. God pouring out His Holy Spirit was Him restoring the image that was lost when Adam and Eve fell. This outpouring of God's Spirit saw a restored spiritual authority and dominion, but more so the indwelling presence of God by which we cry Abba Father.

In saying that the day had fully come (fulfilled, accomplished), means that God sovereignly chose this particular day to be what all of the previous Pentecost were and more. In other words, the event described here in **Acts 2** was divinely ordained in the past to happen at this particular time and place. All of the Jewish celebrations of the holiday to this point pointed to this day, something which is known as typology. All of the Jewish celebration of the second harvest pointed to this day in which God appointed it to be the second harvest. As we shall see, the harvest would include both Jew and Gentile. It would be the celebration of a worldwide harvest of souls and not just those in Palestine. When the Scripture says I will pour out my Spirit upon all flesh, it doesn't mean everyone is going to be filled with God's Spirit. Instead, it means God will pour out His Holy Spirit on every nation. As was evident in **Acts 2:5** [5] *And there were dwelling at Jerusalem Jews, devout men, out of every nation under heaven.* People from every nation under Heaven were strategically gathered in Jerusalem on the Day of Pentecost. This reminds us of the prophecy that God spoke to Abraham. In thee shall all the nations of the earth be blessed. God is such a unique and loving God. He desires to see people from every nation be saved and so shall it be. This Gospel must be preached to the four corners of the earth and then the end will come.

The outpouring of God's Holy Spirit on the Day of Pentecost was not just a fulfilment of **Proverbs 1 and Joel 2** but also the fulfilment of a prophetic act that took place in **John 20**. **John 20:21-23** [21] *Then said Jesus to them again, Peace be unto you: as my Father hath sent me, even so send*

I you. *²² And when he had said this, he breathed on them, and saith unto them, receive ye the Holy Ghost: ²³ Whose soever sins ye remit, they are remitted unto them; and whose soever sins ye retain, they are retained.* This was shortly after Jesus was resurrected from the grave. The disciples all went back to their old ways. Some of them forget the prophetic words Jesus spoke about His death but also how He would arise from the grave after 3 days. God is about to restore somebody like the prodigal son by breathing upon them anew. Somebody had lost hope, had lost faith in God. In **Acts 2:1-4**. *The sound from Heaven and the Mighty rushing wind was Jesus Christ breathing upon His church. He was regenerating (restoring His Image and likeness) them.* God first breathed on man in **Genesis 2:7** *⁷ And the Lord God formed man of the dust of the ground and breathed into his nostrils the breath of life; and man became a living being (soul).* Without God we are nothing and spiritually dead. **Job 33:4** *"The Spirit of God has made me, and the breath of the Almighty gives me life.* The baptism of the Holy Spirit is Christ breathing on us and the purpose of this is to regenerate us. We must be born of the water and the Spirit. Without the Spirit of Christ, we are none of His. A church without the Holy Spirit is a dead church. Pastors and leaders without the Holy Spirit are dead. Like the Valley of dry bones in **Ezekiel 37** we need the breath of God to breathe on us and in us. **Ezekiel 37:9-10** *⁹ Also He said to me, "Prophesy to the breath, prophesy, son of man, and say to the breath, 'Thus says the Lord God: "Come from the four winds, O breath, and breathe on these slain, that they may live."* ¹⁰ *So I prophesied as He commanded me, and breath came into them, and they lived, and stood upon their feet, an exceedingly great* *army*. It wasn't until the breath which signifies God Spirit breathed on the bones then they came alive. It wasn't until Jesus breathed on the apostles with the outpouring of the Holy Spirit, they quickened and empowered themselves to be effective witnesses of the resurrection of the Lord Jesus Christ.

The outpouring of God's Spirit on the Day of Pentecost brought a revival that was never seen before. It was the birth of the Church of the Lord Jesus Christ; the beginning of the Last Days and three thousand souls were added to the Church. The Apostles were mistaken to be drunk with natural wine but instead they were filled and empowered by the Holy Spirit to go into all the world to be a witness of the resurrection of Jesus Christ from the dead. Being filled with the Holy Spirit, Peter was able to boldly preach and declared the word of God as the Spirit gave him utterance. He was able to declare the path of salvation to all those who were under the sound of his voice. Peter became a mighty preacher as he was filled with the Holy Spirit. With that power and incisiveness, he drove home the truth of their responsibility for the death of Jesus Christ, intensified by the fact that every Messianic claim was established by the resurrection. It was a profound Biblical sermon, Biblical in the true sense of the word, that became the sword of the Spirit that pierced the hearts and consciences of the people. How much of the preaching of today needs to get back to Pentecost. It will then be the preaching that convicts and converts.

The Spirit-filled Church, the church on its knees praying, Spirit of burning come, has but one message for a lost world.

I Will Pour Out My Spirit Unto You

It is to that church the awakened sinner will find his way. With the Holy Spirit pricking their hearts they'll ask as was asked at Pentecost, "What shall we do?" It was to this Peter responded by saying **Acts 2:38-44** [38] *. . . Repent and be baptised every one of you in the name of Jesus Christ for the remission of sins, and ye shall receive the gift of the Holy Ghost.* [39] *For the promise is unto you, and to your children, and to all that are afar off, even as many as the Lord our God shall call.* [40] *And with many other words did he testify and exhort, saying, Save yourselves from this untoward generation.* [41] *Then they that gladly received his word were baptised: and the same day there were added unto them about three thousand souls.* [42] *And they continued steadfastly in the apostles' doctrine and fellowship, and in breaking of bread, and in prayers.* [43] *And fear came upon every soul: and many wonders and signs were done by the apostles.* [44] *And all that believed were together and had all things common.*

To truly preach the message of salvation and be effective witnesses in these End Times we must be filled with and be led by the Holy Spirit. True salvation according to the Scripture starts with genuine repentance as people are convicted by the Holy Spirit upon hearing the Gospel of the Lord Jesus Christ. After repentance they should obtain water baptism in the Name of Jesus Christ or the Name of the Lord Jesus, shortly after they will receive the gift of the Holy Ghost. The promise of the Holy Spirit was not just for those on the Day of Pentecost, but this promise is to all those who are far off and as many as the Lord God shall call. The person reading this book is one of those who are afar off and who the Lord God has called. What was evident was before the outpouring of the Holy Spirit there was unity and after the outpouring of the Holy Spirit the Church continued steadfastly in the apostles' doctrine in unity, fellowship, breaking of bread and in prayers. They had all things in common. The true Church of Jesus Christ is a united body that has order and oneness according to the Holy Scriptures and is led by the Holy Spirit.

The need for our understanding to be opened to the Scriptures

Luke 24: 30-32,44-49 [30] *And it came to pass, as he sat at meat with them, he took bread, and blessed it, and brake, and gave to them.* [31] *And their eyes were opened, and they knew him; and he vanished out of their sight.* [32] *And they said one to another, did not our heart burn within us, while he talked with us by the way, and while he opened to us the scriptures?* [44] *And he said unto them, these are the words which I spake unto you, while I was yet with you, that all things must be fulfilled, which were written in the law of Moses, and in the prophets, and in the psalms, concerning me.* [45] *Then opened he their understanding, that they might understand the scriptures,* [46] *And said unto them, thus, it is written, and thus it behoved Christ to suffer, and to rise from the dead the third day:* [47] *And that repentance and remission of sins should be preached in his name among all nations, beginning at Jerusalem.* [48] *And ye are witnesses of these things.* [49] *And, behold, I send the promise of my Father upon you: but tarry ye in the city of Jerusalem, until ye be endued with power from on high.*

The word understanding refers to; the power to comprehend, superior power of discernment; enlightened intelligence: knowledge of or familiarity with a particular thing; skill in dealing with or handling something. Understanding also refers to having insight and awareness.

God said to Solomon in reference to **2 Chronicles 1:11-12** *"Because this was in your heart, and you have not asked riches or wealth or honour or the life of your enemies, nor have you asked long life; but have asked wisdom and knowledge for yourself, that you may judge My people over whom I have made you king; (12) wisdom and knowledge are granted to you; and I will give you riches and wealth and honour, such as none of the kings have had who were before you, nor shall any after you have the like."*

Solomon advises us to follow in his footsteps in praying for wisdom, knowledge, and understanding. He notes that if we do; like him, we too will receive honour, promotion, grace, and glory.

Proverbs 4:1-2, 5, 7 *[1] Hear, ye children, the instruction of a father, and attend to know understanding. [2] For I give you good doctrine, forsake ye not my law. [5] Get wisdom, get understanding: forget it not; neither decline from the words of my mouth. [7] Wisdom is the principal thing; therefore, get wisdom: and with all thy getting understand.* We are told in verse 1 to attend to know understanding. That means we need to listen or be present in order to know understanding. At times we can be physically present in an audience, but we are absent in spirit and soul. Messages are being spoken but we are not tuned in because even though physically present, our soul and spirit haven't attended. Therefore, we will not be able to listen to understand. There are many times the Holy Spirit is speaking but we are unable to listen to what He is saying to the Church because our spirit is not in tuned to the Holy Spirit. Whoever has an ear to hear let them hear what the Spirit is saying to the church.

Solomon said that wisdom is the principal (main, most important) thing. However, he also tells us in all our getting we need to get understanding. Wisdom and understanding goes hand in hand, like oxygen and hydrogen in order to produce water. Wisdom is the ability to make the right judgement of situations. However, if we lack the insight or awareness which is what understanding is, we won't be in a position to make the right decisions. This is what God desires of us, to be able to make the right decisions always. However, we must have an awareness and an insight into situations to be able to do this successfully. Therefore, when we pray for God to give us wisdom we should also pray for understanding as well.

Proverbs 3: 13-15,19-20 [13] *Happy is the man that finds wisdom, and the man that gets understanding.* [14] *For the merchandise of it is better than the merchandise of silver, and the gain thereof than fine gold.* [15] *She is more precious than rubies: and all the things thou canst desire are not to be compared unto her.* [19] *The Lord by wisdom hath founded the earth; by understanding hath he established the heavens.* [20] *By his knowledge the depths are broken up, and the clouds drop down the dew.* According to this passage when we find wisdom and get understanding we will be happy. Wisdom is something that has to be discovered and understanding is something that is given. The Lord Jesus Christ instructed the Jews to "search the scriptures; for in them ye think ye have eternal life: and they are they which testify of me." It is in the process of searching the Scriptures that God will impart understanding to us.

When we have wisdom and understanding, the value of silver, gold and rubies can't be compared to them. There are people in this life that have great riches but lack Godly wisdom and understanding. Not only is wisdom the principal thing but it was by this God who founded the earth. Therefore, wisdom is foundational and is the foundation that bears the weight of structures. However, it was by understanding God established the Heavens. We can start something, but it would be no good if we can't sustain or maintain it. This is one of the benefits of having understanding, we are able to establish and sustain the things God has given to us. Some people start a church organisation, but they are not able to sustain it because they lack understanding. It is in the multitude of counsellors that the purpose is established. In counsel understanding is imparted. **Proverbs 24:3-4** [3] *Through wisdom is an house builded; and by understanding it is established:* [4] *And by knowledge shall the chambers be filled with all precious and pleasant riches.* These verses confirm that it is by wisdom things are built, but it takes understanding to establish (prove) them. The Scripture tells us in 2 Timothy to study to show ourselves approved. This means without the understanding of the Scriptures God won't approve us as his Ministers. In other words, we won't have a ground to stand on or no foundation.

Solomon prophetically wrote in chapter one of Proverbs "if you turn at my reproof, behold I will pour out my Spirit and make known my words to you." The Lord Jesus Christ before He was ascended did two very important acts. Firstly, he breathed on the apostles which was symbolic of the outpouring of the Holy Spirit on the Day of Pentecost. Secondly here in **Luke 24** He opened their understanding that they may understand the Scriptures. God has in mind not only for us to be filled with the Holy Spirit but that we also understand the word of God. Jesus who was the Word in Flesh or the Living Word was with the Apostles, and they didn't realise who He was until their eyes were opened. Their heart burned within them when He opened the scriptures to them. Until God opens our understanding to the Scriptures, we won't be able to understand prophecies and other aspects of Scripture, nor will we be able to "rightly divide the word of truth."

Like Elisha prayed for God to open the eyes of his servant in order for him to see in the Spirit realm, God wants us to pray to Him to give us the spirit of wisdom & revelation in the knowledge of Him, that the eyes of our understanding be enlightened. When this is done, we will know what the hope of His calling is and what are the riches of the glory of His inheritance in the saints. **Ephesians 1:17-18** [17] *I pray that the God of our Lord Jesus Christ, the Father of glory, may give unto you the spirit of wisdom and revelation in the knowledge of Him,* [18] *the eyes of your understanding being enlightened, that ye may know what is the hope of His calling, and what are the riches of the glory of His inheritance in the saints.*

It is in having knowledge of the Holy One that understanding will be imparted to us. In obtaining this knowledge and wisdom it all comes down to fearing God. Fearing God means to reverence and worship Him instead of being afraid of Him. **Proverbs 9: 9-10** *[9] Give instruction to a wise man, and he will be yet wiser: teach a just man, and he will increase in learning. [10] The fear of the Lord is the beginning of wisdom: and the knowledge of the holy [Holy One] is understanding.* In society we have many skilful scientists and other people. However, many of them don't fear God and lack the knowledge of the Holy One. Therefore, they lack the understanding that God desires for us to have. They think because they have knowledge of science, they know everything. What they don't realise is the science they know is very limited knowledge compared to having knowledge of the Holy One who is omniscient. *This means God is all science, He is all knowing, He is all knowledge.* **Daniel 1:3-4,8** *[3] And the king spake unto Ashpenaz the master of his eunuchs, that he should bring certain of the children of Israel, and of the king's seed, and of the princes; [4] Children in whom was no blemish, but well favoured, and skilful in all wisdom, and cunning in knowledge, and understanding science, and such as had ability in them to stand in the king's palace, and whom they might teach the learning and the tongue of the Chaldeans. [8] But Daniel purposed in his heart that he would not defile himself with the portion of the king's meat, nor with the wine which he drank: therefore, he requested of the prince of the eunuchs that he might not defile himself. [17] As for these four children, God gave them knowledge and skill in all learning and wisdom: and Daniel had understanding in all visions

and dreams. [19] *And the king communed with them; and among them all was found none like Daniel, Hananiah, Mishael, and Azariah: therefore, stood they before the king.* [20] *And in all matters of wisdom and understanding, that the king enquired of them, he found them ten times better than all the magicians and astrologers that were in all his realm.*
Daniel 2:19-22 [19] *Then was the secret revealed unto Daniel in a night vision. Then Daniel blessed the God of heaven.* [20] *Daniel answered and said, blessed be the name of God for ever and ever: for wisdom and might are his:* [21] *And he changes the times and the seasons: he removes kings and sets up kings: he giveth wisdom unto the wise, and knowledge to them that know understanding:* [22] *He reveals the deep and secret things: he knoweth what is in the darkness, and the light dwelleth with him.*

The Scripture above says that Daniel purposed in his heart not to defile himself with the king's meat. This shows that Daniel and the three other Hebrew boys feared God. Reiterating the words of Solomon above that the fear of the Lord is wisdom and the knowledge of the Holy One is understanding, confirms why Daniel and the others were ten times smarter than the great magicians, astrologers in the realm of Babylon. God gave them the ability to be skilful in all wisdom, cunning in knowledge and understanding all science. Because of his fear for God, Daniel was given the ability also to understand all visions and dreams. David said in the book of Psalm that the secret of the Lord is with them that fears Him. This is so true, Joseph when he was in Egypt feared God and God gave him the ability like Daniel to interpret the king's dream. God is a revealer of deep and secret things, however He will only give this ability to those who fears Him.

There are many so-called pastors, archbishops, bishops, prophets, apostles, evangelists, teachers and preachers who try to expound the word of God. However, because they lack a genuine relationship in which they walk in the fear of God, they don't have the ability to rightly divide the word of truth. If they are going to be in a position to rightly divide the word of truth, they need to first start walking in the fear of God. Secondly like the apostles they need God to open their understanding that they might understand the scriptures. Unless God opens our understanding, it will remain locked, and we won't be able to understand the scriptures.

There are many so-called men and women of the Church whose understanding is shut and are preaching or teaching God's word ineffectively. They then end up wrongly dividing the word of truth and causing problems and confusion for themselves and others. God is not the author of confusion. There are many people being led astray to the pit of Hell with itchy ears and an addiction to false doctrines. Some people believe because they wear a religious robe, a ring, a cross etc they qualify to rightly divide God's word. The anointing to unlock our understanding is not found in any of these things but in the Lord Jesus Christ Himself. Many are called but few are chosen. It is the chosen ones who have answered the call of God, walking in the fear of the Lord, that God has opened their understanding that they might understand the Scriptures.

I don't subscribe to this ideology that every church organisation is of God and therefore we can all "come together and be united." Behold, how good and how pleasant it is for brethren to dwell together in unity! People can gather in the same place, but they are not together in unity. The blessing will flow when the people are together in unity. The Holy Spirit was poured out when the one hundred and twenty were in one accord in the Upper Room on the Day of Pentecost. The Church that the Lord Jesus Christ birth was a united body whose steps were ordered by the word of God and led by the Holy Spirit. Their steps being ordered in God's word meant there was an order to their lifestyle, unlike the many indiscipline in church organisations today, yet they profess to be Christians. In these church organisations any and anything goes but not in the church that the Lord Jesus Christ birth. **Ephesians 4:3-6** *³ Endeavouring to keep the unity of the Spirit in the bond of peace. ⁴ There is one body, and one Spirit, even as ye are called in one hope of your calling; ⁵ One Lord, one faith, one baptism, ⁶ One God and Father of all, who is above all, and through all, and in you all.*

Acts 2:41-47 *⁴¹ Then they that gladly received his word were baptised: and the same day there were added unto them about three thousand souls.*

⁴² And they continued steadfastly in the apostles' doctrine and fellowship, and in breaking of bread, and in prayers. ⁴³ And fear came upon every soul: and many wonders and signs were done by the apostles. ⁴⁴ And all that believed were together and had all things common; ⁴⁵ And sold their possessions and goods, and parted them to all men, as every man had need. ⁴⁶

And they, continuing daily with one accord in the temple, and breaking bread from house to house, did eat their meat with gladness and singleness of heart, ⁴⁷ *Praising God and having favour with all the people. And the Lord added to the church daily such as should be saved.*

The Apostles whose understanding were opened to understand the Scriptures, preached the undiluted word of God as they were inspired by the Holy Spirit. Thousands of souls daily were baptised and added to the church. There is a power and authority that flows when the word of God is rightly divided by someone who's understanding is open to understanding the Scriptures. In the same breath of the word of God being rightly divided by the Apostle Peter, many souls were baptised, the people continued steadfastly in the apostles' doctrine (teachings of the Scripture), fellowship (love, united), breaking of bread (holy communion, food), and prayers. Fear (reverence for God and the presence of God) came upon every soul and many wonders and signs were done by the apostles. They continued daily in one accord in the temple. Have we ever asked the question why we don't see the power of God flowing in our church organisations as it did in the inception of the true Church of the Lord Jesus Christ?

If we are going to experience the same results, we need to get back to the original foundation that was laid by the apostles in Scripture. We need to get back to the apostles' doctrine and continue steadfastly in it. We need to be in fellowship and unity, breaking bread, singleness of heart. We need to Endeavour to keep the unity of the Spirit in the bond of peace. Having the knowledge there is one body, and one Spirit, even as ye are called in one hope of your calling. One Lord, one faith, one baptism (water baptism in the Name of the Lord Jesus or Jesus Christ as the apostles did throughout the book of Acts) One God and Father of all, who is above all, and through all, and in you all. It is then we are going to experience continuous revival of souls being saved, added to the church, and being disciplined to maintain their faith in Christ. This is a foundation check. What foundation is the church organisation you are a part of founded on? If it's not according to the apostles, it's not of Jesus Christ. There are many church organisations who don't teach and are afraid to teach from The Book of Acts (because they don't understand it and it contradicts their doctrines). **1 Corinthians 3:11** [11] *For other foundation can no man lay than that which is laid, which is Jesus Christ.* **Ephesians 2:20-22** [20] *And are built upon the foundation of the apostles and prophets, Jesus Christ himself being the chief cornerstone;* [21] *In whom all the building fitly framed together grows into an holy temple in the Lord:* [22] *In whom ye also are builded together for an habitation of God through the Spirit.*

Who do you say That I the Son of man am?

Matthew 16:13-20 [13] *When Jesus came into the coasts of Caesarea Philippi, he asked his disciples, saying, who do men say that I the Son of man am?*

[14] *And they said, some say that thou art John the Baptist: some, Elias; and others, Jeremias, or one of the prophets.* [15] *He*

saith unto them, but whom say ye that I am? ¹⁶ *And Simon Peter answered and said, Thou art the Christ, the Son of the living God.* ¹⁷ *And Jesus answered and said unto him, blessed art thou, Simon Barjona: for flesh and blood has not revealed it unto thee, but my Father which is in heaven.* ¹⁸ *And I say also unto thee, that thou art Peter, and upon this rock I will build my church; and the gates of hell shall not prevail against it.* ¹⁹ *And I will give unto thee the keys of the kingdom of heaven: and whatsoever thou shalt bind on earth shall be bound in heaven: and whatsoever thou shalt loose on earth shall be loosed in heaven.* ²⁰ *Then charged his disciples that they should tell no man that he was Jesus the Christ.*

The Lord Jesus posed the question to his disciples, who do men say I the Son of man am? The response from the disciples were all names of prophets. This showed the people had partial knowledge of who He was. By the works He did they were able to compare Him to previous prophets. The Lord Jesus Christ was the Great High Priest, King of kings and a Prophet. However, He was more than this. The common thing for the disciples then was to go with the common knowledge of the people. How much time in church organisations people limit themselves to the knowledge of God and the things of God because they hold dear to the doctrine of men, rather than choosing to seek God for themselves. How much time God wants us to pursue the deeper depths and the higher heights in Christ but we fall short because we like to quote what a so-called pastor, bishop, Bible College or Bible Seminary said rather than searching the Scriptures for ourselves. **Acts 17:11** *These (Berean Brethren) were more noble than those in Thessalonica,* *in that they received the word with all readiness of mind, and searched the scriptures daily, whether those things were so.* It's good that people can; received God's word with all readiness, quote the preachers but like the Berean brethren God wants us to search the Scriptures daily to see if the things we hear are correct. God's word is the blueprint and should be our measuring stick.

Amidst the various opinions of who Jesus was; Peter was able to tune into the Spirit and when he did, the Father in Heaven gave him a Divine revelation that Jesus was the Christ, the Son of the Living God. When Jesus posed the question, He asked who do men say that I am the Son of Man? Son of man is referring to His humanity. However, His intention was for them to go beyond the natural and see His Divinity as the Christ, the Son of the Living God. Peter was the only one who was locked into this and saw not only His humanity but most importantly His Divinity. Christ (means anointed). The title, the Anointed One, corresponds to the Messiah, the Hebrew name. It is the Greek translation of the Hebrew word. With the word "the" prefixed, i.e., the Christ, it signifies the Messiah of Old Testament prophecy **(Ma 16:16,20; Mk 8:29, Jo 1:41)**. Jesus, the personal name of Christ, given at his birth. Is often used with Christ-Jesus Christ- so that the word Christ becomes practically a part of the proper name **(Jo 1:17, Ac 11:17, Ro 5:1)**. There are some people even today who are still awaiting the first coming of the Messiah. He was amongst them over 2000 years ago and they didn't acknowledge Him because they lack Divine revelation.

At first Jesus asked what the opinion of others about Him was. Then most importantly He asked, who do you say that I am? God wants us to have a personal revelation of who He is. How long are we going to build our salvation on the opinion of others about who the Lord Jesus is? God wants to reveal Himself personally to us this very day. Peter allowed himself to be used by God and in return Jesus pronounced him blessed because flesh and blood did not reveal to him but instead is Father who was in Heaven. Unfortunately, many people fail to obtain the revelation of who the Lord Jesus is because they are looking to flesh and blood. The Lord Jesus said to Peter upon this rock (the Divine revelation of the Lord Jesus) that He would build His Church and the gates of Hell would not prevail against it. He went on to say to Peter, *and I will give unto thee the keys of the kingdom of heaven: and whatsoever thou shalt bind on earth shall be bound in heaven: and whatsoever thou shalt loose on earth shall be loosed in heaven.*

Preceding obtaining the keys of the Kingdom of Heaven is the Divine revelation of who the Lord Jesus is. No Divine revelation, no foundation, and no keys. The keys symbolise the power and authority that we are going to use to counteract the gates of Hell and the Kingdom of darkness. Keys grant us access through doors, gates, and windows. When Adam fell from grace, he conceded these keys to Satan in the Garden of Eden. When Lord Jesus was crucified, He went into Hell and took the keys of death and Hell, but now He is giving us the keys to the Kingdom of Heaven. With these keys to the Kingdom of heaven whatsoever we bind on earth is already bound in Heaven, whatsoever we loose on earth is already loosed in heaven. When we obtain the keys, it's as if earth is aligning to what's already taken place in Heaven. In Heaven God's will is being done eternally. A church organisation that lacks Divine revelation of who the Lord Jesus is, is a powerless church because they don't have the keys to the Kingdom of Heaven.

1 Samuel 3:7,21 *7 Now Samuel did not yet know the Lord, neither was the word of the Lord yet revealed unto him. 21 And the Lord appeared again in Shiloh: for the Lord revealed himself to Samuel in Shiloh by the word of the Lord.* If we are going to have a Divine revelation of who the Lord Jesus is, we need to spend time in God's word. The word of God was not yet revealed to Samuel and neither did he knew the Lord then. After this God appeared to Samuel in Shiloh and revealed Himself to Samuel by the word of the Lord. It is through diligent study of God's word we are going to have the Lord reveal Himself to us. No so-called Bible Seminary or Bible School will bring this Divine revelation, and neither will any number of certificates, letters before our names. But like Samuel the Lord will only reveal Himself Divinely in our personal time of study of His word, and in us diligently pursuing Him. **2 Timothy 2:15** *15 Study to show thyself approved unto God, a workman that need not to be ashamed, rightly dividing the word of truth.* In our diligent study of God's word, we are not showing how others are approved unto God, rather we are showing ourselves approved unto God, and to rightly divide the word of truth. When we diligently study God's word we receive God's approval and we will be skilful to rightly divide the word of truth.

The Lord Jesus being the Christ means He was the Promised Messiah, the Anointed One. The Anointed One means the Spirit of God being upon Him to carry out the mandate of Heaven, eradicating the Kingdom of darkness from people's lives and placing the Kingdom of God within them. Not only was the Lord Jesus the Christ but He was the Saviour of the world. The angels announced His Name Jesus because He shall save His people from their sins. Being the Son of God meaning God in flesh the angels also announced Him as being Emmanuel meaning God with us. In John chapter 14 the Lord Jesus revealed the Father. **John 14:7-11** *[7] "If you had known Me, you would have known My Father also; and from now on you know Him and have seen Him." [8] Philip said to Him, "Lord, show us the Father, and it is sufficient for us."*

[9] Jesus said to him, "Have I been with you so long, and yet you have not known Me, Philip? He who has seen Me has seen the Father; so how can you say, 'Show us the Father'? [10] Do you not believe that I am in the Father, and the Father in Me? The words that I speak to you I do not speak on My own authority; but the Father who dwells in Me does the works. [11] Believe Me that I am in the Father and the Father in Me, or else believe Me for the sake of the works themselves. Jesus declared if the disciples had known Him, they'd also have known the Father. The Father who is a Spirit (God is a Spirit) dwelled in Him and that's what made Jesus God. He went on to say from now on you know Him and have seen Him. To simply put this, if we know the Lord Jesus we know the Father who is God. If we don't know the Lord Jesus, we don't know the Father because the Lord Jesus Christ is the

way, The Truth, and the Life. No one can come to the Father except by Him.

John 17:25-26 *²⁵ O righteous Father, the world hath not known thee: but I have known thee, and these have known that thou hast sent me. ²⁶ And I have declared unto them thy name and will declare it: that the love wherewith thou hast loved me may be in them, and I in them.* After the Father in Heaven revealed to Peter who the Lord Jesus was, Jesus explained to the other disciples who He was. The world doesn't know who the Father is, and neither do they know who the Lord Jesus was. Not because you've seen someone, it doesn't mean you know who they are. **John 1:18** *¹⁸ No man hath seen God at any time, the only begotten Son, which is in the bosom of the Father, he hath declared him.* We cannot see spirit and God is a Spirit. This Spirit was in the Lord Jesus Christ. He declared Him by the works He did. Not only did the Lord Jesus reveal the Father and the works of the Father but He also declared the Name of the Father. It was the same Name the angels declared that Name is Jesus. Yes, the Father has a Name. Father is not a name but a title. Not only was the Lord Jesus and the Father were one, but the Lord Jesus was the Spirit. **2 Corinthians 3:17** *¹⁷ Now the Lord is that Spirit: and where the Spirit of the Lord is, there is liberty.* The one and only Spirit being mentioned here is the Holy Spirit. **Ephesians 4:4-6** *⁴ There is one body, and one Spirit, even as ye are called in one hope of your calling; ⁵ One Lord, one faith, one baptism, ⁶ One God and Father of all, who is above all, and through all, and in you all.* That One Lord is the Lord Jesus Christ.

Matthew 28:16-20 ¹⁶ *Then the eleven disciples went away into Galilee, into a mountain where Jesus had appointed them.* ¹⁷ *And when they saw him, they worshipped him: but some doubted.* ¹⁸ *And Jesus came and spake unto them, saying, All power is given unto me in heaven and in earth.* ¹⁹ *Go ye therefore, and teach all nations, baptising them in the name of the Father, and of the Son, and of the Holy Ghost:* ²⁰ *Teaching them to observe all things whatsoever I have commanded you: and, lo, I am with you always, even unto the end of the world. Amen.* The Disciples worshipped the Lord Jesus because you only worshipped God and by now they knew He was God. At His birth, the wise men from the East saw His star and travelled to Jerusalem to worship Him who was born King of the Jews. Again, they knew He was God in flesh and came to worship Him. When they saw the young child with Mary His mother, they fell down and worshipped Him. The Lord Jesus spoke unto the disciples saying "all power is given unto me in Heaven and earth." If all power is given unto the Lord Jesus Christ it means He had all authority and there would be no power for anyone else unless He delegated it. This again proves He was God manifested in the flesh.

The Lord Jesus then instructed the disciples to "Go ye therefore, and teach all nations, baptising them in the name of the Father, and of the Son, and of the Holy Ghost." "Teaching them to observe all things whatsoever I have commanded you." **Luke 24:45-47** ⁴⁵ *Then opened he their understanding, that they might understand the scriptures,* ⁴⁶ *And said unto them, thus it is written, and thus it behoved (necessary) Christ to suffer, and to rise from the dead the third day:* ⁴⁷ *And that repentance and remission (water baptism)* *of sins should be preached in his name among all nations, beginning at Jerusalem.* In The book of John, the Lord Jesus both declared the Father and the Name of the Father. That Name was and is still Jesus. He was the Word that became flesh and manifested as the Son. The Lord Jesus Christ is the Spirit (Holy Spirit, Holy Ghost). The Lord Jesus Christ taught the disciples to observe all things whatsoever He commanded them. The instruction to water baptise in the Name of the Father, Son and Holy Ghost was a command and they did observe it.

After the Lord Jesus Christ opened their understanding that they might understand the Scriptures they realised there was only one Name by which to baptise people. On the Day of Pentecost, the Apostle Peter who observed this command and had his understanding opened to Scripture, in addition to having the Divine revelation of who the Lord Jesus was, commanded the people in **Acts 2: 37-38** [37] *Now when they heard this, they were pricked in their heart, and said unto Peter and to the rest of the apostles, Men and brethren, what shall we do?* [38] *Then Peter said unto them, Repent, and be baptised every one of you in the name of Jesus Christ for the remission of sins, and ye shall receive the gift of the Holy Ghost.* Peter's understanding of the Scriptures was opened and He realised that since the Lord Jesus was that Spirit and He it was Who declared the Name of the Father, commanded the people to be baptised in water in the Name of Jesus Christ. Other baptisms were done throughout the book of Acts, they were either done in the Name of Jesus Christ or the Name of the Lord Jesus.

A lot of church organisations today, in religious error, conduct water baptism in the "Name of the Father, Son and Holy Ghost," or in the "Name of the Father, Son and Holy Ghost in Jesus Name," (this one shows misunderstanding or confusion. Why come up with your own so-called formula when the Apostles made it plain in the Book of Acts). This clearly shows their understanding has not been fully opened to Scripture and they don't truly understand who the Lord Jesus is. Some people often say, "but aren't they all the same thing?" The answer to that is no and for this very clear and obvious reason. There is not one place found in Scripture where someone who was being baptised in water had "In the Name of the Father, Son and Holy Ghost," pronounced over them. The reason for this is because there is no other name given among men whereby we may be saved. Not only that but the only declaration the Apostles declared during water baptism was the "Name of the Lord Jesus or the Name of Jesus Christ."

This is what we are expected to pattern in our day. Have you ever wondered why the Scriptures teach that whatever we do in words (say) or deeds (actions, practises) we do all in the Name of Jesus Christ?) Most preachers do everything (marriages, funerals, baby dedication, pray etc) in the Name of the Lord Jesus except water baptism. Satan knows this is one of the most powerful practises in Scripture when a person identifies with the Lord Jesus's death, burial, and resurrection but He wants the Name of the Lord Jesus to be silent. He also knows there is no other name given by which we must be saved and that at the mention of the Name Jesus demons tremble and flee. The song writer says "Say the

Name , the Name of Jesus, say the Name so precious, no other Name I know." Going forward and doing God's work He doesn't want us to hold back when it comes to declaring the name of the Lord Jesus Christ in everything we do, even if it means we are imprisoned for the most powerful Name yet the Name (Jesus Christ) that brings the most offence in the Universe.

Like many soldiers in the Gideon army, at the water, a lot of church organisations have gotten water baptism wrong (I'm not writing to insult, disrespect or pull down anyone but rather to reveal God's heart of love and truth). God's truth is not partial truth but rather truth that is one hundred percent as is written, practised and manifested in Scripture. We start where the Scriptures start and finish where they finish. The Holy Spirit has impressed upon my heart that if we are going to experience a revival of souls in these end times we must get back and preach water baptism and baptism of the Holy Spirit as it was done in the Book of Acts. Sadly, a lot of church organisations belittle water baptism and baptism of the Holy Spirit and don't preach them as they should. There are people ministering in church organisations and they have not yet been water baptised. A person's entrance into the Church of the Lord Jesus Christ is through water baptism. In the inception of the church many people were added daily to the church because water baptism was preached with conviction and the Apostles understood the importance of it. **1 Corinthians 3:6** *⁶ I have planted, Apollos watered; but God gave the increase.* The revelation that comes from this verse as it relates to water baptism and souls being added to the church is this.

The planting is the preaching of the word, and the watering is the baptism of souls. The souls being added daily to the church is God giving the increase. However, in order for there to be watering (water baptism) there must first be planting (preaching of the word, seeds being sown) and in order for God to give the increase (souls being added to the church daily) there must be watering of the seeds (water baptism). But God expects us to do it like the Apostles did in the Book of Acts. Now you know why a lot of church organisations are empty. Even some of those who appear to have the crowd the manifestation of the power of God is not evident because we have wrongfully divided the word of truth.

There is great power in the Name of the Lord Jesus. **Acts 4:10-12** [10] *Be it known unto you all, and to all the people of Israel, that by the name of Jesus Christ of Nazareth, whom ye crucified, whom God raised from the dead, even by him doth this man stand here before you whole.* [11] *This is the stone which was set at nought of you builders, which is become the head of the corner.* [12] *Neither is there salvation in any other: for there is none other name under heaven given among men, whereby we must be saved.* **Colossians 3:17** [17] *And whatsoever ye do in word or deed, do all in the name of the Lord Jesus, giving thanks to God and the Father by him.* Here we are instructed that whatsoever we do in words or actions it is to be done in the Name of the Lord Jesus. Principalities and powers recognise this great Name. **Philippians 2:5-11** [5] *Let this mind be in you, which was also in Christ Jesus:* [6] *Who, being in the form of God, thought it not robbery to be equal with God:* [7] *But made himself of no reputation, and* *took upon him the form of a servant, and was made in the likeness of men:* [8] *And being found in fashion as a man, he humbled himself, and became obedient unto death, even the death of the cross.* [9] *Wherefore God also hath highly exalted him and given him a name which is above every name:* [10] *That at the name of Jesus every knee should bow, of things in heaven, and things in earth, and things under the earth;* [11] *And that every tongue should confess that Jesus Christ is Lord, to the glory of God the Father.* **Colossians 1:13-20** [13] *Who hath delivered us from the power of darkness, and hath translated us into the kingdom of his dear Son:* [14] *In whom we have redemption through his blood, even the forgiveness of sins:* [15] *Who is the image of the invisible God, the firstborn of every creature:* [16] *For by him were all things created, that are in heaven, and that are in earth, visible and invisible, whether they be thrones, or dominions, or principalities, or powers: all things were created by him, and for him:* [17] *And he is before all things, and by him all things consist.* [18] *And he is the head of the body, the church: who is the beginning, the firstborn from the dead; that in all things he might have the preeminence.* [19] *For it pleased the Father that in him should all fullness dwell.*

[20] *And, having made peace through the blood of his cross, by him to reconcile all things unto himself; by him, I say, whether they be things in earth, or things in heaven.* The Bible tells us in Genesis 1 that in the beginning God created the Heavens and the Earth. Here in Colossians 1 we are told that all things were created by Him (the Lord Jesus Christ). This would also conclude that the Lord Jesus was God manifested in flesh as the Son of God. The Apostles were beaten and

imprisoned because they disobeyed the command not to speak at all or teach in the Name of Jesus **(Acts 4:17-18)**. Phillip preached the Kingdom of God and the Name of Jesus Christ and people believed and were baptised **(Acts 8:12)**.

Even as some people read this chapter, they are still unclear about who the Lord Jesus is. Just like Samuel if you pray and spend time in the Scriptures the Lord will reveal Himself to you. The secret of the Lord is with them that fears Him. The secret things of God are a mystery, but they can be revealed. **I Timothy 3:16** ¹⁶ *And without controversy great is the mystery of godliness: God was manifest in the flesh, justified in the Spirit, seen of angels, preached unto the Gentiles, believed on in the world, received up into glory.* **John 20:27-28** ²⁷ *Then saith he to Thomas, reach hither thy finger, and behold my hands; and reach hither thy hand, and thrust it into my side: and be not faithless, but believing.* ²⁸ *And Thomas answered and said unto him, My Lord and my God.* The disciple Thomas was with the Lord Jesus for three years. He concluded that Jesus was both Lord and God.

Acts 7:59-60 ⁵⁹ *And they stoned Stephen, calling upon God, and saying, Lord Jesus, receive my spirit.* ⁶⁰ *And he kneeled down and cried with a loud voice, Lord, lay not this sin to their charge. And when he had said this, he fell asleep.* On the verge of his death, Stephen called upon God saying, "Lord Jesus", receive my spirit. This again shows that God who is the Father has a Name. Whenever a person is calling out to someone, they would mention that person's name. On this occasion Stephen mentioned both God's title and His Name, Lord Jesus.

Someone said, "there is something special about the Name of Jesus." All the Heavens knows it, those who are redeemed know it and the demons tremble at it. In Matthew 6 the Lord Jesus taught His disciples to pray . . . Our Father who art in Heaven. Hallowed be thy Name . . . The Father in Heaven has a Name and that Name is Hallowed (Holy, Reverenced). That was the Name Christ declared. That Name is the most powerful in the Universe, that Name is wonderful, that Name brings deliverance and healing, yet that Name is the most abused (taken in vain) Name, that Name is Jesus. For at the Name of Jesus Christ, every knee shall bow and tongue confess that He is Lord.

Conclusion

God loves mankind so much He made us in His image and likeness. To the extent even after the fall of man, He didn't condemn us eternally. God instead became like us that we might become like Him when He clothed Himself in flesh and became the Eternal Sacrificial Lamb of God. The purpose of this was to restore fallen men to their first estate as sons and daughters of our Heavenly Father. Where they once operated and walked in the spiritual power and authority that Adam and Eve forfeited in the Garden of Eden.

To everyone reading this book, be encouraged. Don't ever settle for less when there are deeper depths and higher heights in Christ Jesus. God has played His part more than once, it's time for us to do our bit. That is to walk in the fear of God and keep His commandments. It is then we will experience the great "Outpouring" God has for us.

A fresh wind of the Holy Spirit is about to blow, and I'm reminded of a very powerful song my late Bishop in Jamaica, Neville George Hamilton (aka Pastor Hamilton or Uncle Neville) used to sing. "Wind of the Spirit blows on me, oh breath of God please let me see. The glory of your majesty. Wind of the Spirit blows, wind of the Spirit blows. Wind of the Spirit blows on me, oh breath of God please let me see. The glory of your majesty. Wind of the Spirit blow, wind of the Spirit blow." This song I believe was written in one of the Annual Conventions.

The Rapture of the Church and the Return of the Lord Jesus Christ is fast approaching, no man knows the hour. Our responsibility is to be prepared and be ready like the five wise virgins who had their lamps trimmed and were stocked up with extra oil. The oil signifies the anointing and the power of God.

When Christ returns, He isn't coming for a powerless Church but instead a Church that was born in obedience to the word of the Lord, prayer, and fasting while overflowing in the love of God and the resurrection power of the Holy Ghost like on the Day of Pentecost. The true Church of the Lord Jesus Christ is the most powerful institution in this world. We can only operate in the power God expects us to, only when we are filled and refilled with the Holy Spirit.

Unfortunately, many church organisations are functioning like the five foolish virgins, with insufficient oil (the anointing) and they don't care to have any in reserve. That's the reason they are always begging for others to give them their extra oil (anointing) when God has given everyone of us the ability to seek Him. That we might be filled and refilled, for us to be empowered to carry out the work He has called us to, while being ready for His return.

Conclusion

The Lord Jesus declared "Blessed are those who hunger and thirst after righteousness for they shall be filled." God wants to pour out on all of us, God wants to fill us up with His anointing in these last days but firstly we must have the desire to hunger and thirst (fasting and prayer), that is to seek after His righteousness. If we seek Him, we shall find Him. Who or what are you seeking? Do you desire God? How do you go about seeking God?

Bibliography

- The King James Bible (A.D. 1611)
- The New Analytical Bible and Dictionary of the Bible. Copyright © 1931 and 1964. John A. Dickson Publishing Company Chicago USA.
- Fowler James. A. Man Has God Intended 1998. WWW. ChristIn You .Net.
- God's Covenants -A Teaching Manual of Bible Doctrine (Charles Green, 1976).
- www.ebglobal.org › biblical-articles
- www.padfield.com › 2003
- www.christianity.com
- www.whatsinthebible.com/what-is-pentecost

Coming Soon

BOOKS

- The Outpouring (Volume Two)- Walking In Spiritual Authority As Sons and Daughters of Our Heavenly Father.
- The Voice of Hope- "Poems to Uplift Your Soul"- Volume One and Volume Two.
- The Voice of Hope-"Inspirational Nuggets"- Volume Three

SONGS

- If it wasn't for your grace
- Education

About The Author

Richard Scott Brown was called by God at the tender age of 15 from very humble beginnings. He is (now) an ordained Minister, International Chaplain (Ambassador at Large) and qualified Secondary School Maths Teacher. Richard lives with his elegant wife Anthonette and three beautiful daughters. He is on an 'End Time' mission to spread the unadulterated gospel of Jesus Christ to the ends of the earth. With the hope that, many souls will be saved and delivered to the glory of Almighty God. He seeks to edify and encourage the Body of Christ and others, through his giftings and talents (Teacher & Preacher of the Gospel, poet, and songwriter).

To whom much is given, much is required. Therefore, Richard's ultimate desire in life is to bring glory and honour to the Almighty God. Who came to redeem mankind in the form of the Lord Jesus Christ. This he'll do by tapping into every giftings and talent that God has given him. While making the most of the opportunities he is afforded and walking through every open door according to God's perfect will for his life.

Richard believes we should "buy the truth and sell it not," because it is knowledge of the Truth (Jesus Christ) that is going to bring complete deliverance and freedom to mankind. For Richard the truth is all or nothing, it is not 99.99% but rather 100%. Richard desires to reveal God's truth in its entirety as is revealed through the Holy Scripture and the Holy Spirit to everyone he comes across, and who so desires.

Contact Information:

Email: richardbrown_2001@yahoo.com

Facebook: Richard Scott Brown

Instagram: richard.scott.brown

Twitter: Richard Scott Brown (@Richard92741107)

Printed in Great Britain
by Amazon